NUMBER 346

THE ENGLISH EXPERIENCE

ITS RECORD IN EARLY PRINTED BOOKS
PUBLISHED IN FACSIMILE

NETHERLANDS

THE CONFESSION OF FAYTH

N.P. 1602

DA CAPO PRESS
THEATRVM ORBIS TERRARVM LTD.
AMSTERDAM 1971 NEW YORK

The publishers acknowledge their gratitude
to the Curators of the Bodleian Library, Oxford,
for their permission to reproduce
the Library's copy.

(Shelfmark: 4^0. C. 44Th)

S.T.C.No. 18434
Collation A–G^4, $H^{2(4?)}$

Published in 1971 by
Theatrum Orbis Terrarum Ltd.,
O.Z. Voorburgwal 85, Amsterdam
&
Da Capo Press
- a division of Plenum Publishing Corporation -
227 West 17th Street, New York, 10011
Printed in the Netherlands
ISBN 90 221 0346 3

Certayne Letters / translated into English / being first written in Latine.

Two, by the reverend and learned Mr. Francis Iunius, Divinitie Reader at Leyden in Holland.

The other, by the exiled English Church, abiding for the present at Amsterdam in Holland.

Together with the Confession of faith prefixed: where vpon the said letters were first written.

Esa. 53. 1.
Who beleveth our report, and to whom is the arme of the Lord revealed?

Printed in the yeare. 1602.

R.G. the translatour of M. Iunius his letters: To the Christian Reader.

SVch as of late yeares have rent themselues from the holie service of God, used im the publique congregations and Churches of England, being destitute of any sound wartant from the worde of God, have sought from time to time so much the more earnestly (as the manner of such is) to shroude themselves vnder the shadowe of humane authoritie. Héce it came to passe that Master Francis Iunius, a mã of great learning and godlinesse, was solicited by some of them (as may appeare by these letters ensuing) in the yeare 99. to be a favourer of their erronious opinions and of their vnchristian disordered and vndutifull proceedings: whose answere, being delivered by himselfe to a religious and worshipful knight, and so comming to my handes, I have presumed to communicate with thee, by the motion of some godly and well disposed, hoping that through the blessing of God, and thy prayers it may proove a good meanes to stay such as are wavering, to confirme such as doe stand, and to recover such as are fallen. For although he doe not enter into an exact discussing of the question with arguments, objections, and answeres: yet he vseth a very grave and godly admonition, which is oftentimes of greater fruite, then a long and learned disputation. And whosoever doth diligently studie the booke of God, shal finde, that the holy Prophets & Apostles do in manie places insist upõ a plaine & simple asseveration of the truth rather then vpon multitude of proofs & arguments. Besides, if we observe the story of the holy Martyrs of our own Church & others, we may preceive that by the sound profession of their faith, and suffering for the same, they have glorified God and advanced the kingdome of Iesus Christ aswel as others have done by arguments and reasons. And yet notwithstanding if thou do well obserue these letters of Master Iunius, thou shalt finde in them not vaine and emptie wordes: but waightie and sounde reasons grounded upon the holie Scriptures of God. Thus praying thee to take these first fruites of my poore laboures in this kinde in good part, and beseching god to give a blessing hereunto, I bid thee heartily farewel in the Lord.

Thyne in the Lord, R.G.

The Answer to R. G. his Epistle prefixed before Mr. Junius letters.

SUch as have separated themselves / from the corrupt service of God / used in the publick congregations and parishes of England / being persecuted with afflictions reproches and slanders / both at home and in the land wher now they live exiles: have ben constreyned to publish to the world / the confession of their Christian faith / and causes of their departure from the foresayd English synagogues for clearing of the truth of God / and witnesses of the same / both which were much and many wayes calumniated: More specially they dedicated that litle book to al Christian universities neer about / to be discussed / approved or reproved by the godly learned in them And sending one in particular / to the hands of M. Fr. Iunius, a man of great learning and godlines / dwelling neer unto them / to be by him and the rest of his brethrē of the universitie at Leyden judged of / they received from him a letter lately by one R. G. trāslated and printed in English / whether with the authors consent or not / is yet unknowne: but the copy (as the publisher sayth) was given out by the author himself / who might had done wel to have given a copy of the answer likewise: or if he did / the translator hath not dealt indifferently / to publish one and not an other. How ever it were / al men may see how just and necessary occasion those exiled Christians now have / to print their answer also / which upō the receipt of his Letter they sent unto him / but hitherto have spared to give out any one copy either of his or theirs: whether for doubt of their owne cause / or reverend regard rather of that mā / let the sequel declare / and let the discrete reader by it judge / whether party hath most advantage.

As for the translators censure that they sought to shrowd themselves vnder the shadow of humane authoritie, this brief narratiō of the cariage of the matter / and the plaine apologie which they make unto Mr Junius of their proceedings / wil shew it (unto al godly wyse) to be but the surmise of a malicious hart. And were it not that the weaknes and badnes of their cause compelleth them thus to doe / it might seem strange that any of the church of England would publish such a writing as this in their owne defence / as if it approved their estate / and condēned those foresayd Christian exiles: when any / whose eyes ar in his head / may see by Mr Junius his writing unto them / as Christian brethren / and refusing at al to undertake the maintenance of those English parishes / or conviction of such as separate from them / how far it is frō justifying those synagogues estate. Yea al wiseharted may and will (we doubt not) easily discerne / how naked and helplesse they be which neither by their friends at home / nor the most learned abroad can otherwise be relieved / then by such things as hitherto they have printed. Or howsoever this present generation shall judge of these things / yet the ages to come / (which wil be lesse partial) wil easily give sentence.

The better to certify thee (good reader) of the whole cause / and cariage therof / here is with these Letters / set forth also their Confession of faith / with the Epistle and preface / as it is in Latine. And wheras ther is since that time published also a second epistle of Mr. Junius / ther is now the answer to it set forth likewise: which answer was presently written upon the receipt of his Letter / but not then sent for causes partly before noted / and now more fully signified and sent to Mr. Junius him self. The things which here are mentioned of corruptions in some other churches / and dealings that have passed about thē / ar yet spared from being published in print at large / til further occasion and provocation be. Onely the general and brief heads of the matter in controversie / ar now printed (as they were sent unto Mr. Junius) although we were loth to do it but that their was neces-

sarie

sarie occasion given by things which passed in the Letters/ as al mē may see. Moreover it is not to be omitted / how in the printed copy of Mr. Junius Letter/ *some things were corrupted/ by alteration/ omission/ and c. Otherwise then in the original by himself first sent/ they do stand and ar yet to be seen. This it is not likely Mr. Junius himself would doe/ but was (perhaps) the printers fault/ or rather indeed the translators evil mind/ for his mother churches advantage/ whō falshood seeketh to uphold/ when syncerity and truth hath forsaken her. It shal therfore rest upon him / as the first fruits of his evil labours in this kind, til he clear himself

*For proof herof see Mr. Iunius owne words noted in the margine of his letter herafter folowing, and compare also this edition of it, with the translators before published.

The Apostles and Prophets / and Martyrs by him mentioned/ dealt not so. Neither yet did they alwayes insist upon a plaine and simple asseveration of the truth, but mainteyned it also with proofes and arguments from scripture / and sound reason/ against such as oppugned the same. Act.17.2.3. and 18.28. and 28.23. Rom,1.17. and 3.4.10. and 4.3.7.17. and 9.7.9.12.13.17.20.25.27.29.33. and 10.5.11. 15.19.21. and 11.2.9.26. 1 Cor. 15.3.4.25.27.45.54.55. Gal.3.6.8.10.11.13.22. and 4. 21.22.27.30. Esa.40.12. and 41.21.22.23.24. and 44.6. and c. Mal. 4.4. Acts & monuments in the historie of Mr. Brute, Thorp, Lambert, Ridly, Philpot, Bradford, and many others. And though the Apostles and Prophets had / yet no mās asseveratiō now/ may be compared with theirs/ but must be tried by their writings. And so these Christian exiles / published to that end their faith unto the world / against which to this day/ neither Mr. Junius nor any els of that or the other universities/ have to our knowledge used any one weighty and sound reason grounded vpon the holy scripture of God, as this translator would bear men in hand he doth / and as the Prophets did in al their asseverations / taking their ground from the law before given. Mat.22.40. The Lord rebuke Satan/ and make bright the glorie of his name and Gospel / and turne to the profit of every faithful soule / these things now published by his unworthy and contemned servants/ to his owne eternal prayse in Christ, Amen.

To the

To the Reader.

By the Printers default there are (good Reader) a few faults escaped in the printing/some whereof are here noted. Which with the rest thou observest thy self/we pray thee amend/thus.

Pag.11.lin.13.then to make. Pag.12.l.8.all that.
Pag.15.l.20.21.22.32.33.34.blot out these marcks:* ‡ ((* " ‡.
Pag.16.l.1.also * of old. And lin.7.Iob.1.6.
Pag.17.l.3.vnwritten.And blot out/of men.
Pag.18.l.13.Act.3.22. Pag.24.l.34.Eph.4.11.
Pag.25.l.20.Rev.2.1. 1.King.12. Pag.27.l.28.Gal.3.28.29
Pag.29.l.1.no whit. L.18.1.Tim.2.2.L.49.Exod.18.12. and 20.18.
Pag.39.l.7.Churches of this city/that etc.and then be delivered. L.27.contend.
Pag.40.l.26.publish. Pag.41.l.1. their private Confessions of faith their apol.L.7.8.prevaile.
Pag. 42.l.22.let vs. Pag.45.l.13.ingenuously.
Pag.47.in the margent.l.10.licet vobis.And l.13.discindere.
P.48.l.10/cõsent.P.50.li.9.evẽ to strive earnestly.P.51.l.32.taunting.
Pag.53.l.3.yea so. L.13.many weak ones/before so many deadly.
Pa.54.l.1.Anist.is such/ as being but one/yet it meeteth in three severall places :whereupon it is so confus.etc. And li.32. Gal.4.10.11.

Note besides/where Mr.Iunius in his second letter (Pag.47.) pretendeth/ as if there had ben some fault in the Messenger or vs that he knew not to whom or whither he should have written his first: that in the book it self which was delivered vnto him/there was particular mention both of the place and of the partyes from whõ it came:as may be seen in the Epistle prefixed before it/ which is of the dedication to the vniversityes. And els how knew he at the moneths end more then before/ to whom and whither to send as he did? Which poynt is so very playne / as to himself we thought there needed not then so much as any mention of it. Yet thought we here to note it/least some others not observing so much/ might thinck the fault wherof he speaketh to ly on vs or the messẽger/which (what soever it were) is still to rest vpon himself/for ought we know.

The Confession of faythe of certayne English people, living in exile, in the Low countreyes.

Together vvith the Preface to the Reader which we wish of all may be read and considered.

2. Cor. 4/13.
We beleev: therefore have we spoken.

Harmony of Confess. in the preface set before it, in the Name of the French aud Belgick Churches.

The Prelates and Priests do alvvay cry out, that vve are Hereticks, Schismaticks, and Sectaryes. Hovvbeit let thē knovv, that the crime of Heresy is not to be imputed to thē, vvhose faith doth vvholy rely vpon most sure grounds of the Scripture; That they are not Schismaticks, vvho entierly cleave to the true Church of God, such as the Prophets and Apostles do describe vnto vs: Nor they to be counted Sectaryes, vvho embrace the truth of God vvhich is one and alvvayes like it self.

To the reverend and learned men, the Students of holy Scripture, in the Christian Vniversities of Leyden in Holland, of Sanctandrewes in Scotland, of Heidelbergh, Geneva, and the other like famous scholes of learning in the Low countreyes, Scotland, Germany, and France.

The English exiles in the Low countreys, wish grace and peace in Iesus Christ.

THis true confession of our faith, in our judgment wholy agreable to the sacred Scripture, we do here exhibit vnto all to be discussed: and vnto you (reverend Sirs) we dedicate it for two causes. First, for that we know you are able in respect of your singular knowledge in the Scriptures, and hope you are willing in respect of your syncere piety, to convince our errours by the light of Gods word, if in any thing we be out of the way. Secondly, that this testimony of Christian faith, if you also fynd it agree with the word of truth, may by you be approved, eyther in silence or by writing, as you shall think best.

It may be, we shalbe thought very bold, that being despised of all, yet doubted not to sollicite you so many and so great learned men. But this we did, partly at the request of others to whom we would not deny it: partly with desier to have the truth through your help better defended and further spread abroad: partly cōstreyned by our exile and other calamityes almost infinite: partly also moved with love of our native cōutrey, and of these wherein now we live, and others else where: wishing that all may walk with a right foot to the truth of the Gospell, and praying daily vnto God, that the great work of restoring Religion and the Church decayed, which he hath happily begun in these latter tymes, by our Gracious Soveraigne and the other Princes of these countreyes and ages (his servants) he would fully accomplish, to the glory of his name and eternall salvation in Christ of his elect in all places of the earth.

As for the causes which moved vs to publish this Confession of faith, and to forsake the Church of England as now it stādeth, we have truly and as briefly as we could related them in the Preface to the Reader, hereafter following: and therefore thought here to omit the repetition of them. The Lord Iesus alway preserve you and your Vniversityes to the praise of his name, the ornamēt of good learning, the propagation and maintenance of his pure Religion. From Amsterdam in the low countreyes. The yeare of the last patience of the saints, 1598.

The preface to the Christian Reader.

IT may seeme strange unto thee (Christian Reader) that any off the Englysh nation should for the truth of the Gospell be forced to forsake their natyve contrye, and lyve in exile, especially in these dayes, when the Gospell seemeth to have free passage, and florish in that land. And for this cause have our exile bene hardly thought of by many, and evil spoken of by some, who know not (as it seemeth) eyther the trewe estate of the Church of England, or causes of our forsaking and separating from the same, but hearing this sect (as they call it) to be every where spoken against have (with out all further search) accounted and divulged us as heretickes, or Schismatickes at the least. Yea some (and such as worst might) have sought the increase of our afflictions, even here also yf they could, which thinge they have, both secretly and openly attempted. This hath Sathan added unto all our former sorrowes, envying that we should have rest in any part of the b inhabyted world, and therfor ceaseth not to make warre with the remnant of the womans seed, which keepe the commaundemēts of God and have the testimony of Jesus Christ. But the Lord that c brought his former Israell out off Egypt, and when they walked aboute from nation to natiō, from one kingdome to an other people, suffered no man to do them wronge, but reproved kinges for their sakes: the same Lord yet lyveth to mayntayne the right off his afflicted servantes, whome he hath severed, and dayly gathereth out off the world, to d be unto himselff a chosen generatiō, a royall priesthood a peculiar people and Israell off God: He e is our hope and strength and helpe in trobles ready to be found, he will hyde us under his winges, and under his feathers we shall be sure untyll these myseries be over past. And though we could for our partes well have borne this rebuke off Christ in silence, and left our cause to him who iudgeth iustly all the children off men: yet for the manyfestation and clearing of the truth off God from reproche off men, and for the bringing off others togither with our selves to the same knowledge and fellowship off the Gospell, we have thought it needfull and our duty to make knowen unto the world, our unfeyghned fayth in God, and loyall obedience towardes our Prince, and all Governours set over us in the Lord, together with the reasons off our leaving the ministery worship and Church off England. Which are not (as they pretend) for some fewe faultes and corruptions remayning, such as we acknowledge may be found in the perfectest Church on earth: Neyther count we it lawfull for any member to forsake the fellowship off the Church for blemyshes and imperfections, which every one according to his calling should studeously seeke to cure, and to expect and further it untyll eyther there followe redresse or the disease be growen incureable, and the f candlestick be moved out off the place. But we having through Gods mercy learned to discerne betwixt g the true worship off God, and the Antichristian leitourgie, the true ministerie off Christ and Antichristian priesthood and prelacy, the ordinances off Christes testament, and popysh cannons: have also learned to leave h the evill and choose the good, to forsake Bavell the land off our captyvitie, and get us unto Sion the mount of the Lordes holynes, and place where his honour dwelleth.

Act. 28, 22
b Rev. 12.
c Psal. 105, 13, 14.
d 1 Pet. 2, 9.
e Psal. 46, 1.
f Apoc. 2, 5.
g 2 Cor. 6, 14, 15, &c.
Psal. 94, 20.
2 Thes. 2, 3.
h Psa. 37, 27
Ier. 51, 6.
Rev. 18, 4.
& 14, 1.

But first we desyre thee, good Reader, to understand, and mynde that we have not in any dislyke of the civill estate and politicke goverment in that common wealth, which we much lyke and love, seperated our selves from that Churche: Neyther have we shaken of our alleageance and dutyfull obedyence to our Soveraigne Prince Elezabeth, her honorable Consellers, and other Magistrates set over us, but have alwayes and still do reverence love and obey them every one in the Lord, opposing our selves against al enemyes forreigne or domesticall: against

all invasions/insurrections/treasons or conspiracies by whome soever intended
against her Majestie and the State/and are ready to adveture our lyves in their
defence/iff need require. Neither have our greatest adversaryes ever bene able to
attaint us of the least disloyalty in this regarde. And though now we be exiled/
yet do we dayly pray and will for the preservation peace and prosperity off her
Majestie and all her domynions

And wheras we have bene accused off intrusion into the Magistrates office/as
Neh.6.6. goeing about our selves to reforme the abuses in that land/it is a mere malicious
7.8. calumnie/which our adversaries have forged out of their owne hart. We have alwayes both by word and practise shewed the contrary/ neyther ever attempted
or purposed any such thinge: but have indevored thus onely to reforme our selves and our lyves according to the rule off Gods word/by absteyning from all e-
vyll and keeping the commandements off Jesus: leaving the suppressing and casting out off those remnants of Idolatry unto the Magistrates/to whome it belongeth.

And further we testifye by these presents unto all men and desyre them to take
knowledge herof that we have not forsaken any one poynt of the true ancient ca-
tholicke and apostolicke fayth professed in our land: but hold the same groundes
of Christian religion with them still/agreeing lykewise herein/ with the Dutch/
Scottysh/Germane/French Helvetian/and all other Christian reformed Churches round about us/ whose confessions publyshed/ we call to witnes our agre-
Harmon. of ment with them in matters of greatest moment/being cōferred/with these articles
confess. of our fayth following. The thinges then onely against which we contend/and
which we mislyke in the Englysh parish assemblyes/ are many reliques of that
man off Synne (whome they pretend to have abandoned) yet reteyned among
them/and with a high hand mayntayned/upholden/and imposed. The parti-
culers wherof being almost infinite) cannot well off us heere sett downe/and would
be tedious and yrksome to thee (good Reader:) But the principall heades we wil
truely relate/and that so briefely as in so large and confuse a subject we can.

First/in the planting and constituting of their Churche (at the begining of our
Queene Elizabets reigne) they receved at once into the body of that Churche/as
members/the whole land/which generally then stood for the most part professed
i1 Pet.2,5. Papistes who had revolted from the profession/which they made in the dayes of
Ier.51,26 king Edward off happy memorye/ and shed much blood off many Christian
k.Act.2,38 Martyrs in Queene Maryes dayes. This people yet standinge in this fearfull
40,41 & 8, sinfull state/in idolatry/blyndnes supersitiō and all manner wickednes/without
36.37 & 15 any professed repentance/and without the meanes theroff namely the preaching
9. Ioh.10, off the word goeing before/were by force and auctority of lawe onely compelled/
3.4.5. and together receved into the bosome and body of the Church: their seed bapti-
Esa.35,8.9 sed/themselves receved and compelled to the Lords supper/ had this ministery
1Ioh.15,2.5 and service (which now they use) inioyned and set over them/and ever synce they
Mat 18,15,17 and their seed remayne in this estate/ being all but one body comonly called the
Lev.13,46. Church of England. here are none exempted or excluded/be they never so propha-
Numb,4.13 ne or wretched/no athiest/adulterer/thiefe or murderer/no lyer/periured/witche or
m Ioh 15, coniurer and c. all are one fellowship one body/one Churche. Now let the law off
19.and 17. God be looked into/and there wilbe found/ that such persones i are not fit stones
14,16. for the lordes spiritual howse/ no meete members for Christes glorious body.
Mat.3,12 k None of these may be receved into the Churche without free professed fayth re-
Lev.20,24 pētance and submission unto the Gospell of Christ and his heavenly ordynances:
26. Neyther may any contynew l there longer then they bring forth the fruytes off
1.Ioh.4.5.6 fayth walking as becometh the Gospell of Christ. Christ m Jesus hath called and
severed his servants out of and from the world. How then should this confused
and

and mixed people be esteemed the orderly gathered true planted and right constituted Church of God.

Secondly as they have reteyned the whole rout of the poppish multitude without any distinction, for members of their Churche so have they set over them (as reason was) the same poppish Clergie and Prelacy, which they receved from the Romysh Apostasie and this day is to be found in the poppish Churches: to witt, Archbs, Primats, Bbs, Metropolitanes, Suffraganes, Archdeacōs, Deanes, Chauncellors, Commissaries, and the rest of that rable, which rule and governe these assemblyes according to the poppish cannons, rites, and customes. These have the power and aucthoritie in their hādes to set forth iniunctions, to make and depose ministers, to excommunicate both priest and people which they do very exquisitly if they yeld not unto them their due homage and obedience: These have both Ecclesiasticall and civill aucthoritie, to reigne as Princes in the Churche and lyve as Lordes in the common wealth, to punysh, imprison, and persecute evē to death all that dare but once mutter against their unlaufull proceedinges. Of these prelates tyranny cruelty and unlawfull aucthoritie the better sort both of preachers and people have cryed out, and longe tyme sued unto the Prince and parliamēt to have them removed out of the Churche, as being the lymmes of Antichrist. But not prevayling they are now content (for avoyding of the crosse of Christ) to submitt them selves and their soules to this Antichristian hierarchie, and beare the sinfull yoke and burthen of their traditions, and to receve and carry aboute the dreadfull and detestable marke of the beast upon them.

About forty ecclesiastical popish offices are at this daye in the Churche of Englād never a one appointed by Christ in his testament.

Apoc. 13.

Thirdly, The inferiour ministery of that Churche, consisteth of Priests, Parsons, Vicars, Curats, hired preachers, or Lecturers, with Clarkes, Sextons, &c. all which have receved their offices callings and aucthoritie from their forenamed Lordes the Prelats, to whome they have sworne their canonicall obedience, and promysed to performe it with all reverence and submyssion. Their office is to read over the servyce booke and Bps. Decrees, thereby to worship God, to marry, to bury, to church women, to visit the sicke give him the Sacrament, and forgyve him all his sinnes: and if their lyvinges or benefices (as they are called) amount to a certeyne summe of money in the Queenes booke, then must they preach, or get some other to preach for them fower sermons in a yere in their parish, where also must be noted that the most part of these Priestes are utterlye unlearned, and cannot preache at all: wherby it cometh to passe that most of the people are as blynde as they were in the darke dayes of popery. These ministers generally, aswel preachers as other, lyve in feare and servitude under their foresaid Lords the Bbs. for as without their lycence wrytten and sealed they cannot preach, so upon their displeasure and for not obeying their iniunctions, they are many tymes suspēded degraded, and if they will not be ruled, put in prison: so that sundry of them have bene suspended and imprisoned for preaching against the Prelats, not subscribing to their devised articles and booke of cōmon prayer, not wearing the square capp and surplis, not reading the service booke, and be tyed to the same not coming to the Bishops courtes, visitations, inquisitions, and c. tyll now of late being wearyed with these trobles, they give place to their tyranny, and are content to conforme themselves, and yelde their canonicall obedience according to their oathe, keeping now silence yea going back, bearing and bolstering the thinges, which heretofore by word and wryting they stoode against so longe as there was any hope that the Queene and Counsell would have harkened unto them, and put these adversary Prelats out of the Churche.

VVith what words & rites, in what habit & gesture, these things are to be done, they are taught in their rubrik

Fourthly, for the administration, which is by lawe imposed upon all both Clergie and Laitie, (for so they distinguish them) they have gathered their service booke verbatim out of the masse booke, turning out of latine into englysh the Suffragies

fragies

fragies, Prayers, Letany, Collects, &c. (leaving out some of the grosse pointes therin) keeping still the old fashyon of Psalmes/ Chapters/ Pistles/ Gospells/ versicles/ respondes/ also Te Deum, Benedictus, Magnificat, Nunc dimittis, Our Father, Lord have mercy vpon vs, The Lord be with you, O Lord open thow my lyps, Glory to God on high, Lyft vp your harts, O come let vs rejoyce, Glory be to the Father, Quicunque vult, &c. These doe they read dayly morning and evening all the yere longe in their priestly vestures/ Surplus/ cope/ and c. some they saye/ and some they singe having in their Cathedrall Churches/ the Organs, Queristers, singing men and boyes as in tymes past in popery. Many poppish errors yet remayne in that booke/ which their owne preachers have noted/ and found fault with. There are they prescribed what prayers to read over the dead/ over the corne and grasse/ some tyme in the yere. By it are they inioyned to keepe their holy dayes to their Lady (as they call her) to all Saincts and Angells/ to all Christes Apostells/ (except Paul and Barnabas) whose eves they are commaunded to fast/ as also their Lent and Ember dayes/ besydes frydayes/ and satardayes through out the whole yere. By this booke are the ministers instructed how to marry with the signe of the Ringe/ and c. to baptise in the hallowed Font with signe of the crosse/ with Godfathers and Godmothers/ asking the childe whether it will forsake the devyll and all his workes/ and c. to minister also their other sacrament or communion to the people kneeling/ as when in popery they receved their maker/ the wordes of Christes institution altered and others in stead of them take out of the popes portuis/ with innumerable such lyke enormyties and fopperies wherewith it swarmeth. And this is all the worship and service which many parishes have contynually/ except peradventure some wrytten homelyes which the unlearned priestes read unto them. This service must first be read/ and hath the preeminence/ even on the Lordes dayes before any preaching yea before the Bible it self. He that can read this booke distinctly is fit ynough with them to be a priest/ yea many that have ben Artificers/ as Shoemakers/ Taylers/ Weavers/ Porters/ and c. and with out any giftes or knowledge at all/ save only to read Englysh/ have bene and are admytted and to this day mayntayned by the prelats in the ministery. To these Churches ministers and servyce must all the people there come every daye/ yea though they have in the next parish a preacher/ and in their owne a dumbe unlearned priest/ yet are they all tyed to their owne Church/ and minister/ and must at the least twise a yere, receve the Sacrament at his handes. If they refuse this/ or do not ordinaryly come to their parish Churche/ then are they summoned/ excommunicated/ and imprisoned/ tyll they become obedient. In this bōdage are our countrymen there held under their Priests and Prelats: and such as by the word of God witnes against and condemne these abhominations/ they hate punysh put to death and persecute out of the land. Who now in whome any sparke of true light is cannot playnly perceive this their ministery worship and Churche to be false and adulterate? doth Christes eternall testament ordeyne and approve of suche popish Lordes and Prelats to reigne over his Churche? are these those Christian Bishops/ that is o Pastors/ Teachers and Elders/ which he hath set in his Churche and over his owne people unto the worldes end? Or can those preachers which are thus created and deposed by/ thus sworne and obediēt unto their spirituall lordes/ be deemed true teachers of the Gospell of Christ lawfully called and ordeyned to that ministerye? Is that their Englysh Masse the trewe and p spirituall worship of God according to his owne wil? we are taught in the scriptures q that there can be no agrement made betwixt Christ and Antichrist/ betwixt the Lawes of God and mens traditions: that the servants of Jesus may not submytt unto or receve the marke of that beast/ neyther drinke of the cup of the whore of Babylons fornycations/ or buy any of her wares: but must

contend

Some of them in certaine English books set forth, have reckned above 100. popish corruptions yet reteyned in this church.

o Rom. 12
1. Cor. 12.
Eph. 4.
p Iohn. 4, 24
Mat 15, 9
q Deu 6, 4, 5
Mat. 16, 6
2. Cor. 6, 14
15
Psal 106, 34
35. 36.

s contend for the mayntenãce of that faith/which was once gyven vnto the saints/ keeping their soules and bodyes pure from Antichristian pollutions/ touching t no vncleanethinge u nor having any fellowship with the vnfruteful workes of darknes/ w least by partaking with their synnes they receve also of their plagues/and drincke of the wyne of the wrath of God / and be tormented in fyre and brimstone before the holy Angells and before the lambe for evermore. — s Iude:ver.3 · t 2 Cor.6, 17. · u Eph.5,11. · w Reb.18,4 & 14,10,11.

If Christ be God let vs follow him: but if the pope be God/what shall wee say? why have we left him / his Church and ministery / his worship and jurisdiction/ or what halting/and mocking with the Lord is this / to put away the popes person and retayne his prelacy and ministery/his Lawes/Traditiõs and Cannons/ his worship and service:or at the least to frame vnto our selves a worship ministery and Church after the patterne and mould of the Apostacye of Roome/which what other thing is it/them to make an Image of that first wild beast / and force men to worship it? — Mat.6, 24. · x 2.King. 16,10,11,12. · Apoc,13,12 14,15.

Thus seest thow briefely (good Christian Reader) the thinges which we mislike in the Churche of England / and for which we have separated our selves / as God commandeth. To all these/if we were amongst them/ should we be forced to submytt our bodyes and soules / or els suffer violence at the handes of the Prelats/and end our lyves by violent death or most miserable imprisonment / as many of our bretheren before vs have donne. For so great is the malice and power of those romysh priests/that they persecute vnto death such as speake against them: and such poore Christians as they cast into their noysoms pryson/ can seldome or never get out (except with shipwracke of cõscience) vntyll they be caryed forth vpon the Bere. Neyther is there any care taken for their relieffe in this case: but being thus cast into pryson / there they are deteyned without any allowance of meate or money for their mayntenance/be their want and poverty never so great. If they have any thing of their owne/ there they are driven to spend it vp: if they have nothing / there they are left by the Prelats to feede on the ayre . And that they maye more readily be sterved / or weakened in the truth / they are comonly shut vp in close prison/their frends and acquayntance being not suffered to come at them: Nay even their wyves and children being kept and debarred from them by the tyranny of these bloddye Prelats and their instruments : whose hard hartes and vnnaturall cruelty/if thou didest vnderstand (gentle Reader) as many of vs have felt / and to this daye yet feele it would make thy hart to bleede/ considering their vnmercyfull and barbarons dealing. And how many soules have perished in their prisons through miserable vsage/how many have ben put to death and how many banyshed / though we could to their eternall infamy relate to all the world/yet wil we not blaze abroad their acts (for we take no delight in laying open their shame) but mourne for them in secret / commytting our cause to God that judgeth justly/knowing that he z that maketh inquisition for blood remembreth it / and will not forget the complaint of the poore. And thou (Christian Reader) voutch safe to remember vnto God in thy prayers such as yet remayne in bandes and pryson amongest them for the testymony of Jesus / enduring a hard fight of afflictions/ and having the sentence of death in them selves are lyke (if the Lord send not vnexspected delyverance) there to end their dayes. — y Ier.51,6. · Mich.2,10. · Rev.18,4. · 2 Cor.6,17. · Act.2,40. · z Ps.9.12. · Heb.13,3.

Concerning our selves who through the mercy of God have found a place of rest in this land / for which benefyt we are alwayes and every where humbly thanckfull: we desyre (Christian Reader) thy charitable and Christian opinion of/ and holy prayers vnto God for vs/ whose kingdome we seeke / whose ordinances we desyre to establysh and obey : protesting with good consciences / that it is the truth of his Gospell only for which we stryve against those cursed reliques of Antichristian apostasie:vnto which we dare in no wise submytt our selves/no not for

a moment

a moment. For if it be not lawfull for Christians at this daye to reteyne the cere-
A Gal.4.4.5 monyes of Moses Lawe together with the Gospell/as the Passeover/Circumci-
6.& 5.1.2. sion/the Priesthood/Sacrifices/and c. which yet were once commaunded by God
Heb.8. &9 himself: how can we thincke it tollerable to observe the odious ceremonyes of
& 10.chap. Antichrist/or submytt our selves to his lawes/ Priesthood/ Hierarchie and tradi-
tions/ which the Lord never allowed/and which never entred in to his hart: yea
which he hath so severely forbydden/ with fearefull judgements threatned unto
all that shall so do. But because we have bene very grievously slādred in our owne
nation/and the bruit thereoff hath followed us unto this land/ wherby we have
bene hardly deemed of by many without cause/ we have bene forced at length to
publysh this briefe but true confession of our fayth/ for the cleering of our selves
from sclander/ and satisfying of many who desyred to knowe the thinges we
hold. Wherein if in any thinge we erre (as who is so perfit that he erreth not) we
crave (good reader) thy Christian brotherly censure and information/ promysing
alwayes (through the grace of God) to yeild unto the truth when it shall be further shewed us/ and leave our errors when by the light of his word they shalbe
reproved. In lyke manner it shall be thy part and duty to acknowledge and submytt unto the truth/ by whome soever it is professed/looking allwayes rather to
the preciousnes of the treasure it self then to the basenes of the vessells which con-
2.Cor.4,7 teyne it/or the infirmities of those that witnes the same/in whose mortall bodyes
thow shalt see nothing but the markes and dyeing of our lord Jhesus Christ.
Iam.2,1 But hold not thy fayth in respect of mens persons/ neyther be thow moved at
the evyl reports wich have bene raised of us: Here hast thow the trewe summe of
our Christian fayth try all thinges by the true light of Gods word: and if thou
shalt reape any profit by these our labours/gyve God the glory/ and remember
us unto him in thy prayers. Farewell in Christ Jesus. 1596.

THE CONFESSION OF FAITH OF CERTAINE ENGLISH PEOPLE, IN THE LOW COVNTREYES, EXILED.

Wee beleeue with the heart, & confes with the mouth:

That there is but * one God, one Christ, one Spirit, one Church, one truth, one Faith, one true Religion ‡ one rule of godlines and obedience for all Christians, in all places, at all tymes, to be observed. * Deut. 6. 4. 1 Tim 2. 5. Ep he. 4. 4. 5. 6. 1 Cor. 8. 6. & 12. 4. 5. 6. 13. Ier. 6. 16. Ioh. 14. 6. ‡ 1 Tim. 6. 3. 13. 14. Mat. 15. 9. & 28. 20. Deut. 4. 2. 6. & 12. 32. 1 Cor. 4. 17. & 14. 33. 2 Tim. 3. 15. 16. 17. Gal. 1. 8. 9. Reuel. 22. 18. 19.

2 God is a ✱ Spirit, whose ‡ beeing is of himself, and giveth beeing, moving, and preservation to all other things, beeing himself ☾ eternall, most holy, every way infinit, in greatnes, wisdome, power, goodnes, iustice, truth etc. In this Godhead there be ✱ three distinct persons coeternall, coequall, and coessentiall, beeing every one of them one and the same God, and therefore not divided but distinguished one from another by theyr severall and peculiar propertie: The ✱ Father of whom are the other persons, but he of none; the Sonne ‡ begotten of the Father from everlasting, the holy ☾ Ghost proceeding from the Father and the Sonne before all beginnings. ✱ Ioh. 4. 24. ‡ Exod. 3. 14. Rom. 11. 36. Act. 17. 28. ☾ 1 Tim. 1. 17. Esa. 6. 3 & 66. 1. 2. * 1 Ioh. 5. 7. Mat. 28. 19. Prou. 8. 22. Heb. 1. 3. Phil. 2. 6. 1 Cor. 8. 6. Micah. 5. 2. Psal. 2. 7. Gal. 4. 6. Ioh. 1. 1. 2. 18. & 10. 30. 38. & 15. 26. Heb. 9. 14.

3 God ‡ hath decreed in himself from everlasting touching all things, and the very least circumstances of every thing, effectually to work and dispose them according to the counsell of his owne will, to the glory of his name. And touching his cheefest creatures, GOD hath in Christ ‡ before the foundation of the world according to the good pleasure of his will, " foreordeyned some men and Angels, to eternall lyfe to be ‡ accomplished through Iesus

Jesus Christ, to the ‡ prayse of the glorie of his grace. And hath also of old according † to his iust purpose foreappointed other both angels and men, to eternall condemnation, to be accomplished through their owne corruptiō and desert to the praise of his iustice

‡ Esa.46.10. Rom.11.34.35 36. Gen.45.5.6.7.8. Mat.10.29.30.Eph.1.11 † Eph.1.3.4.5.6.7.10.11. Mat.25.34 2 Tim.1.9.Act.13.48. 1Tim 5.21. Col.1. 14. 17. 18,19.20 & 2, 10 Joh.1.6. Rev.19.10. 1Thes.5.9. Rom.8.29.30. & 9. 23. Iud.ver.4 & 6.Rom.9.11.12 13.17 18.22. with Exod.9.16. Mal.1.3.Mat.25 41.Iob.4.18. 2 Pet.2.4.12. 1 Pet.2.8. Ioh.3.19. Rom 2.5. Prov.16.4.

4. * In the beginning God made al things of nothing verie good: and † created mā after his owne image and likenes in righteousnes ād holines of truth But * streight waye after by the subtilitie of the serpēt which Sathan vsed as his instrument (himself with his Angels having sinned before and not kept their first estate, but left their owne habitation) first * Eva, then Adam being seduced, did wittingly and willingly fall into disobedience and trāsgressiō of the commaundement of God. For the which, death † came vpon all and reigneth over all: yea even † over infants also which have not sinned after the like maner of the trangression of Adam, that is, actually: Hence also it is, that † all since the fall of Adam, are begotten in his owne likenes * after his image, being conceyved and formed in iniquitie, and so by nature children of wrath and servants of sinne, and subiect to death, and al other calamities due vnto sinne in this world and for ever.

* Gen.1.chap. Col.1.16. Heb.11.3. Esa.45.12. Rev.4 11. ‡ Gen 1.26.27. Eph.4.24, Col.3.10. Eccle.7.31.* Gen.3.1.4.5. 2Cor.11.3.* 2Pet.2,4. Iud.ver.6. Ioh.8.44. * Gen.3.1 2.3.6. 1 Tim.2.14 Eccle.7.31. Gal.3.22. † Rom.5.12.18. 19. & 6.23. with Gen.2.17. † Rom.5.14.& 9.11. * Gen.5.3. & 6.5. Psal.51 5. Eph.2.3. Rom.5.12. Deut.27.26. & 28.15. &c.

5 All mankind being thus fallen and become altogether dead in sinne, and subiect to the eternall wrath of God, both by originall and actuall corruption: Yet the elect all and onely, are redeemed, quickned, raysed vp and saved againe, not of themselves, neyther by works (lest anie man should boast himself) but wholly and only by GOD of his free grace and mercy, through faith in Christ Jesus † who of God is made vnto vs wisdome, and righteousnes, and sanctification, and redemption, that according as it is written Hee that reioyceth may reioyce in the Lord.

* Gen.3.15 Eph.1.3.--7.& 2.4.--9. 1 Thes.5.9. 1 Pet.1.2.3.4.5. Gen.15 6.with Rom.4.2 3.4.5.6.22.23.24.25. Act.13.38.39.48. Rom.3.24.25, 26. 2Tim.1 9 Phil.3.8.9.10.11. † 1 Cor.1.30.31 2 Cor.5.21. Ier.23.5.6. & 9.23.24

6 This therfore is lyfe eternall to know the only true God, and whom hee hath sent into the world Jesus Christ. And on the contrarie the † Lord will render vengeance in flaming fire vnto them that know not God, and which obey not the Gospell of our Lord Jesus Christ.

* Ioh.17.3. Heb.5.9. Ier.23.5.6. † 2 Thes.1.8. Ioh.3 36.Zep.1.6

7. Now

7 Now the rule of this knowledge faith and obediẽce, concerning the worship ãd service of God and all other christiã duetyes, is not mens opinions devises, lawes constitutions or traditions unwritten whatsoever, of men, but onely the written word of God conteyned in the canonicall bookes of the old and new Testament.

Ioh.5.39.2 Tim.3.15.16.17. Deut.4.2.5.6. Gen.6.22. Exod.20.4.5 6.& 39. 42.43.1 Chro.28.19. Psal.119.in the whole Psal. Esa.8.19.20.&29.13. Math.15.9. Col.2.8.18.23. Luc.16.29.30.31. Gal.1.8 9. 2.Petr.1.16.19.& 3.2. Reve.22.18.19

8. In this word Jesus Christ hath plainely reveled whatsoever his father thought needfull for vs to know, beleeve and acknowledge as touching his person and Office, in whom all the promises of God are yea, and in whom they are Amen to the prayse of God through vs.

Deu.18.18 Act 3.22.23. Heb.1.1.2. & through the epistle. Ioh 1.1.14 18.& 12 49.50.& 15.15.& 20.31. Pro.8.8.9.& 30.5.6.2. Tim.3.15.16.17,2. Cor.1.20.

9. Touching his person, the Lord Jesus, of whom, Moses and the Prophets wrote, and whom the Apostles, preached, is the †everlasting Sonne of God the father by eternall generation, the brightnes of his glorie, and the engravẽ forme of his Person, coessẽtiall coequal, and coeternall, God with him and with the holy Ghost: By whõ hee made the worlds, by whõ hee upholdeth and governeth all the works hee hath made: Who also, †whẽ the fulnes of tyme was come, was made man of a woman, of the Tribe[a] of Judah, of *the seed of David and Abraham, to wyt, of Mary that blessed Virgin, by the holy Ghost comming upon hir, and the power of the most high overshadowing hir: and was also ‡in al things lyke unto vs, sinne only excepted.

* Genes 3.15.& 22,18,& 49.10, Dan.7.13,& 9.24,25.26. Ier,23,5.6. Psal.2.2. 6.7.12.& 16.10. & 110 with luk,24 44, Ioh.5,46. Act.10.42 .43. & 13 . 33. & c &17.3. ‡ Prouer:8.22. Mich.5.2 , Ioh,1.1.2 3.&.12.37.—41, with Esa.6,1-10 & with Act 28.25 Heb. 1,cap Col,1.15.16,17.& 2.9. †Gal.4 4. Gen.3.15. [a] Heb. 7.14. Reve.5. 5. with Gen, 49. 9, 10. *Rom. 1. 3. & 9.5 Gen 22.18. Gal.3,16. Mat.1.1.&c. Luk:3.23:& c: Esa:7:14: Luk:1:26:and c: Heb.2.16. ‡ Heb.4 15. Es.53.3.4.9. Phil.2.7 8.

10. Touching his Office, Jesus Christ *only is made the Mediator of the new Testamẽt, even of the everlasting Covenant of grace betweẽ God & mã to be perfectly and fully the Prophet, Priest and King of the Church of God for evermore.

1 Tim.2 5. Heb.9.15.and.13.20 Dan.9.24.25. Ioh.14 6. Act.4.12. †Heb.1. 2.& 3,1.2.3.& 7,24.& 12.24.--28, Psal.110.1.2.4.&45. Deu.18.15:18: Esa:9:6:7: Act:5.31: Esa.55:4: Dan:7:13.14. Luk.1.32.33.

11 Unto this office hee was from everlasting, by the iust and sufficient authoritie of the father, and in respect of his manhood from the womb, called and seperated ãd † anoynted also most fully and abũdãtly with all necessary giftes, as it is written: God hath not measured out the Spirit unto him.

* Pro.8.23. Esa.42.6. and49.1.5. Heb.5.5.6. ‡ Esa.11.2.3.4.5.and 61.1.2.3. with Luk.4.17.22. Act.10.38. Ioh.1.14.16, aud 3.34.

12 This office to be Mediator, that is, Prophet, Priest, and King of the Church of God, is so proper to Christ, as neyther in the whole, nor in any part thereof, it can be transferred from him to any other. 1 tim. 2. 5. Heb. 7. 24. Dan. 7. 14. Act. 4. 12. Esa. 43. 11. Luk. 1. 33. Ioh. 14. 6.

13 Touching his †Prophecie, Christ hath perfectly revealed *out of the bosome of his father, the whole word and will of God, that is needfull for his servants, eyther joyntly or severally to know, beleeve or obey: Hee also † hath spoken and doth speake to his Church in his owne * ordinance, by his owne ministers and instruments onely, and not by any false † ministery at any tyme. *Ioh. 1. 18. & 12. 49. 50; and 15. 15. and 17. 8. Deut. 18. 15. 18. 19. Act. 22. 23. 24. Mat. 17. 5. Eph. 1. 8. 9. 2 tim. 3. 15. 16. 17. †Pro. 9. 3. Ioh. 13. 20. Luk. 10. 16. Mat. 10. 40. 41. and 28. 18. 20. Deut. 33. 8. 10. †Mat. 7. 15. 16. and 24. 23. 24. 2 Pet. 2 chap. 2 tim. 4. 3. 4. Rom. 10. 14. 15. and 16. 17. 1 tim. 6. 3. 4. 5. Ier. 23. 21 Ioh. 10. 1—5. Rev. 9. 3. &c.

14 Towching his Priesthood, Christ * beeing consecrated, hath appeared once to put away sinne, by the offring and sacrificing of himself: and to this end hath fully performed and suffred all those things, by which GOD through the blood of that his crosse, in an acceptable sacrifice, might be reconciled to his elect: and having "broken downe the partition wall, and therewith finished and removed all those rites, shadowes, and ceremonies, is now* entred within the vayle into the holy of holiest, that is, to the very heaven, and presence of God, where hee for ever lyveth and sitteth at the right hand of Maiestie * appeering before the face of his Father, to make intercession for such as come unto the throne of grace by that new and living way: and not that onely, but maketh his people a ‡ spirituall howse, and holy Priesthood, to offer up spirituall sacrifices, acceptable to God through him. Neyther doth the Father accept, or Christ offer unto the father any other worship, or worshippers *Ioh. 17. 19. Heb. 5. 7. 8. 9. and 9. 26. Esa. 53. chap. Rom. 5. 19. 1 Pet. 1. 2. 19. Ephe. 5. 2. Col. 1. 20. "Ephe. 2. 14. 15. 16. Dan. 9. 24. 27. Heb. 9. and 10. chap. Rom. 8. 34. Heb. 4. 14. 16. and 7. 25. ‡1 Pet. 2. 5. Revel. 1. 5. 6. & 8. 3. 4. Rom. 12. 1. 12. Mar. 9. 49. 50. Mal. 1. 14. Ioh. 4. 23. 24. Mar. 7. 6. 7. 8. Esa. 1. 12. &c.

Towching

15 Towching his Kingdome, Christ being risen frõ the dead, ascended into heaven, set at the right hand of GOD the Father, having all power in heaven and earth given unto him, he doth spiritually governe his Church: exercising his power† over all Angels and men, good and bad, to the preservation and salvation of the elect, to the overruling and destruction of the reprobate:" communicating and applying the benefits, vertue and fruite of his prophecy and Priesthood unto his elect, namely to the remission, subduing, and taking away of their sinnes, to their iustification, adoption of sonnes, regeneration, sanctification, preservation and strengthning in all their conflicts against Sathan, the world, the flesh, and the temptation of them: continually dwelling in, governing and keeping their harts in his true faith and fear by his holy spirit, which having* once given it, hee never taketh away from them, but by it still begetteth and nourisheth in them repentance, faith, love, obedience, comfort, peace, ioy, hope, and all christian vertues, unto immortalitie, not withstanding that it be somtymes through sinne and tentation, interrupted, smothered, and as it were overwhelmed for the tyme. Agayne on the contrary, †ruling in the world over his enemies, Sathan, and all the vessels of wrath, limiting, using, restrayning them by his mighty power, as seemeth good in his divine wisdome and iustice, to the execution of his determinate counsel, to wit, to their seduction, hardning and condemnation, delivering them up to a reprobate mynde, to be kept through their owne desert in darcknes, sinne, and sensualitie, unto iudgement.

* 1 Cor. 15. 4. et c. 1 Pet. 3. 21. 22. Mat. 28. 18. 19. 20. Psal. 2. 6. Act. 5. 30. 31. Ioh. 19. 36. Revel. 19. 16. Rom. 14. 17. †Iosh. 5. 14. Zach. 1. 8. &c. Mar. 1. 27. Heb. 1. 14. Ioh. 16. 7.---15." Eph. 5. 26. 27. Rom. 5. & 6. & 7, & 8, chap. and 14. 17. Gal. 5. 22, 23. 1 Ioh. 4. 13. &c. *Ioh. 13. 1. and 10, 28. 29. and 14. 16. 17. and 16. 31. 32. with Luke. 22. 31. 32. 40. Rom. 11. 29. Psal. 51. 10. 11. 12. & 89. 30. --34. Iob. 33. 29 30. Esa. 54. 8. 9. 10. 2 Cor. 12 7. 8. 9. Ephes. 6. 10. &c. Gal. 5. 17. 22. 23. †Iob. 1. 6. and 2. chap. 1 King. 22. 19. Esa 10. 5. 15. Rom. 1 21. & 2. 4. 5. 6. and 9. 17. 18. Eph. 4. 17. 18. 19. Esa. 57. 20. 21. 2 Pet 2 chap.

16 This Kingdome shall be then fully perfected when he shall the second tyme come in glory with his mightie Angels to iudge both quick and dead, to abolish all rule, authoritie and power

to put al his enimies vnder his feet, to separate and free all his chosē from them for ever, to punish the wicked with everlasting perdition from his presence, to gather, ioyne, and carry the godly with himself into endlesse glory, and then to deliver up the kingdome to God/ euen the Father, that so the glorie of the father may bee full and perfect in the Sonne, the glorie of the Sonne in all his members, and God bee all in all.

1 Cor.15.24.28.Dan.12.2.3.Ioh.5.22.28.29.Heb,9.28. 2Thes.1.9.10, Mat 13.41.49.et 25,31.1 Thes.4.15.16.17.Ioh.17.21.26.1 Cor.15.28.

17 In the meane tyme, bisides his absolute rule in the world, Christ hath here in earth a* spirituall Kingdome and œconomicall regiment in his Church, which hee hath purchased and redemed to himself, as a peculiar inheritāce. And albeyt that manie hypocrites do for the tyme lurke amongst them, whiles the Church is militant here on earth, yet Christ nothwithstanding [†]by the power of his word gathereth them which be his into the body of his Church, calleth them from out of the world, bringeth them to his true faith/separating them" from amongst unbeleevers, frō idolatrie, false worship, superstitiō, vanitie, dissolute life, and al works of darknes, &c. making thē a royall Priesthod, an holy Natiō a people set at libertie to shew foorth the virtues of him that hath called them out of darknes into his mervelous light, gathering and uniting thē together as* members of one bodi in his faith loue and holy order, unto all generall and mutuall dutyes, †through his spirit instructing ād governing them by such officers and lawes as hee hath prescribed in his word by which Officers and lawes hee governeth his Church, †and by none other.

* Ioh.18.36.1 Tim.2.15.Heb.3.6.9 & 10.21.Zach.4.7. Act.20.28. Tit 2.14. † Mat.13.25.47. & 22.12. Luk.13.25.2 Tim.2.20.. †Mar, 16, 15, 16. Col, 1, 21, 1 Cor, 6.11, Tit, 3, 3, 4, 5. "Esa, 52, 11, Ezra, 6, 21, Act, 2, 40, & 17, 3, 4, & 19, 9, 2Cor, 6, 14,--18, 1Pit.2.4, 5, 9, 25, *Ephe, 4.12, 16, Esa, 60, 4, 8, Psal, 110, 3, Act, 2, 41, Col, 2, 5, 6, †Esa, 59, 21, & 62, 6, 1 Ioh, 2, 27, Ephe, 4, 7, 8, 11, 12, Ier, 3, 15, Ezek, 34, chap, Zach, 11, 8, Heb, 12, 28, 29, Mat, 28, 20, 1 Tim, 6, 13, 14, †Mat, 7, 15, & 24, 23, 24, 2 Tim, 4, 3.4, Ier, 7, 30, 31, & 23, 21, Deut, 12, 32, Revel, 2, 2, & 22, 18, 19,

18 To

18 To this Church hee hath made the *promises, and given the seales of his Covenant, presence, loue, blessing and protectiō: Heere are the † holy Oracles as in the Arke, surely kept and purely taught. Heere are all the †fountaynes and springs of his grace continually replenished and flowing forth, Heere is Christ lifted vp to all Nations, hither hee inviteth all men to his supper, his mariage feast, hither ought ‡ all men of all estates ād degrees that acknowledge him theyr Prophet, Priest and King to repayre, to bee enrolled emongst his houshold seruants, to bee vnder his heavenly conduct and government, to leade theyr liues in his walled sheepfold ād watered orchard, to haue communion heer with the Saincts, that they may bee made meet to bee partakers of their inheritāce in the kingdome of God.

*Lev.26,11,12, Mat,28, 18, 19, 20, Rom,9,4, Esa, 59,20,21, Ezek,48.35, 2 Cor,6,18, ‡Esa.8,16, 1 Tim,3. 15,& 4, 16, & 6,3,5. 2 Tim,2, 15, Tit, 1.9, Deut,31. 26, † Psal, 46.4, 5. Ezek,47,1. &c, Ioh,1,16, &7. 38,39, Ephe,4. 4, 7. "Esa,11, 12, Ioh,3,14, & 12,32, Esa.49.22, *Esa,55,1. Mat,6. 33,& 22, 2.&c. Prov. 9. 4. 5, Ioh, 7, 37. ‡Deut.12.5:11: Esa.2:2:3: & 44.5: Zach.14. 16.17, 18. 19. Act.2,41. 47: Heb, 12 : 22 : &c: Psal: 87 : 5. 6: Song:4: 12: Gal:6: 10: Col:1: 12: 13. Ephe: 2:19.

19. And as * all his servāts and subiects are called hither, to presēt their bodies and soules, and to bring the gyfts God hath given them, so beeing come they are heer by himself bestowed in theyr severall order, peculiar place, due vse, beeing fitly compact and knit togeather by every ioynt of help, according to the effectuall worke in the measure of every part, vnto the edification of it self in love: Wherunto when hee ‡ ascended vp on high he gave gifts vnto men, and distributed them vnto several publik fūctions in his Church, having instituted and ratified to continue vnto the worlds end, onely this publick ordinarie ministery of Pastors, Teachers, Elders, Deacons, Helpers, to the instruction, government, and service of his Church.

*see Article 18. afore : & Exod. 25 2. & 35. 5. 1Cor.12.4,5. 6.7.12.18, Rom,12.4.5,6. 1Pet,4 10. Ephe.4,16, Col,2.5,6,19, ‡Ephe, 4.8, 10,11.12,13, Rom. 12.7. 8. & 16,1. 1Cor 12,4, 5,6.7,8, 11,14,15,16,17,18,28, Act 6,2.3,& 14,23,& 20,17,28, Phil,1,1, 1Pet,5, 1,2,3,4. 1Tim,3,chap, & 5, 3, 9, 17,21, with 6,13,14, Revel.22,18,19, Mat,28,20.

20 This

20 This ministerie is exactely † described, distinguished, limited, concerning their office, their calling to their office, their administration of their office, and their maintenance in their office, by most perfect and plaine lawes in Gods word: which *lawes it is not lawfull for these Ministers, or for the whole Church wittingly to neglect, trangresse, or violate in anie part nor yet to receive anie other lawes brought into the Church by any person whatsoever. †Rom. 12. 7. 8. Ephe. 4. 11. 12. with the Epist. to Tim. and Tit. Act. 6. 3. 5. 6. and 14. 23. and 20. 17. &c. 1 pet. 5. 1. 2. 3. 1cor. 5. 4. et c. and 9. 7, 9. 14. and 12. 4. et c. with Heb. 3. 2. 6. and prov. 8. 8. 9. *Heb. 2. 3. and 3. 3. and 12. 25. et c. 1 Tim. 3. 14. 15. and 6. 13. 14. 2 Tim. 3. 14.—17. Gal. 1. 8. 9. Deu. 4. 2. and 12. 32. Revel. 22. 18. 19.

21. None †may usurp or execute a ministerie but such as are rigtly called by the Church whereof they stand ministers, unto such offices, and in such maner, as God hath prescribed in his word. And being so called, they ought* to give all diligence to fulfill their ministerie, to be found faithfull and unblameable in all things.

†Heb. 5. 4. Num. 16. 5. 40. and 18. 7. 2 chron. 26 18. Ioh. 10. 1. 2 and 3. 27. Act. 6. 3. 5. 6. and 14. 23. Tit. 1. 5. Ier. 23. 21. Num. 8. 9. 10. *Act. 20. 28. 1 Cor. 4. 1. 2. Col. 4. 17. 1 Tim. 1. 18. 19. and 4. 12. and 5. 21. and 6. 11. 12. 13. 14. 2. Tim. 1. 13. 14 and 3. 14. and 4. 5. 1 Pet. 5. 1. 2. 3. 4. Rom. 12. 7, 8,

22. This ministerie is alike given to every Christian congregation, with like and equall power and commission to have and enioy the same, as God offereth fit men and meanes, the same rules given to all for the election and execution thereof in all places. Mat, 28, 20, 1 Cor 4. 17. and 12, 4, 5. 6. 7, and 14, 33, 36, and 16. 1, Eph, 4, 10 11. 12, 13, Revel. 1. 20. 1 Cor, 3. 21, 22, 23. Mat, 18, 17, see besides these, the Article 20. before.

23. As every christian congregation †hath power and commandement to elect and ordeine their owne ministerie according to the rules in GODs word prescribed, and whilest they shall faithfully execute their office, to have them † in superabundant love for their worke sake, to provide for them, to honour them and reverence them, according to the dignitie of the office they execute: So have they also* power and commandement when anie such default, eyther in their lyfe, doctrine, or administration brea-

breaketh out, as by the rule of the word debarreth them from, or depriveth them of their ministerie; by due order to depose them frō the ministerie they exercised: yea if the case so require, and they remayne obstinate and impenitent, orderly to cut them of by excommunication.

‡ Act. 6. 3. 5. 6. & 14. 23. & 15. 2. 3. 22. 23. 2 Cor. 8. 19. 1 Tim. 3. 10. & 4. 14. & 5. 22. Numb. 8. 9. 10. 1 Cor. 16. 3. * 1 Thes. 5. 12. 13. 1 Tim. 5. 3. 17. 18. Heb. 13. 17. 1 Cor. 9. 7. &c. Gal. 6. 6. † 1 Tim. 3. 10. & 5. 22. Rom. 16. 17. Phil. 3. 2. ‡ Tim. 6. 3. 5. Eze. 44. 12. 13. Mat. 18. 17.

24. Christ * hath given this power to receive in or to cut of anie member, to the whole body together of every Christian congregation, and not to anie one member apart, or to more members sequested from the whole, or to anie other congregation to do it for them: Yet so, as ech Congregation ought to use the ‡ best help they can heerunto, and the most meet member they have to pronounce the same in their publick assembly.

* Psal. 122. 3. Act. 2. 47. Rom. 16. 2. Mat. 18. 17. 1 Cor. 5. 4. 2 Cor. 2. 6. 7. 8. Lev. 20. 4. 5. & 24. 14. Num. 5. 2. 3. Deu. 13. 9. ‡ Act. 15. 2. 22. with 1 Cor. 3. 5. 22. & 12. 20. & 14. 33.

25 Every member of ech Christian congregation, how excellēt, great, or learned soever, ought to be subiect to this censure and iudgment of Christ: Yet ought not the Church without great care and due advise to proceed against such publick persons.

Lev. 4. chap. 2 Chro. 26. 20. Psal. 2. 10. 11. 12. & 141. 5. & 149. 8. 9. Act. 11. 2. 4. 1 Tim. 5. 19. 20. 21.

26 As Christ hath for the keeping of this Church in holy and orderly communion, placed some speciall men over the Church, who by their office are to governe, oversee, visite, watch &c. So ‡ lykwise for the better keeping thereof in all places, by all the mēbers, hee hath given authority and layd dutie upon them all to watch one over another.

* Act. 20. 17. 28. Heb. 13. 17. 24. Song. 3. 3. Esa. 62. 6. Ezek. 33. 2. Mat. 24. 45. Luk. 12. 42. 1 Thes. 5. 14. ‡ Mar. 13. 34. 37. Luk. 17. 3. Gal. 6. 1. 1 Thes. 5. 11. Iud. ver. 3. 20 Heb. 10. 24. 25. & 12. 15

27 Finally, whilest the Ministers and people thus remayne together in this holy order and christian communion, ech one endevoring to do the will of God in their calling, and thus to walke to the glory of God, in the obedience of faith, Christ hath promised to be present with them, to blesse and defend them against

D all

all fraud and force of theyr enemyes, so as the gates of Hell shall not prevaile against them.

Mat. 28. 20. Luk. 12. 35. 36. 37. 38. Rom. 16. 19. 20. Deut. 28 1. &c. Zach. 2. 5. & 12. 2. 3. 4. Psal. 125 2 & 132. 13. 13°. &c. Mat. 16. 18.

28 But when and where this holy order and diligent watch was intermitted, neglected, violated: Antichrist that man of sinne did together with other points of Christian faith corrupt and alter also the holy ordinances, offices, and administrations of the Church: and in stead thereof brought in and erected a strange new forged ministery, Leitourgy and government. Yea and the nations kingdomes and inhabitans of the earth were made drunken with this cup of fornications and abominatiõs and all people enforced to receive the beasts marke and worship his image and so brought into confusion and babilonish bondage.

2 Thess. 2. 3. 4. 8. 9. 10. 11. 12. Apoc. 9. and 13. and 17 and 18. cap 1 Tim 4. 1, 2. 3. Psal 74. Esa. 14. 13. 14. Dan, 7, 25. and 8. 10. 11. 12. and 11. 31. 2, Pet 2, Cap, 1 Ioan. 2. 18: 22. and 4. 3. and 2. Ioh. versi, 7. 9.

29 The present Hierarchy retayned and used in Englãd of Archbb. Primates, Lordbisshops, Metropolitanes, Suffraganes, Deanes, Prebendaries, Canons, Peticanons Arch-Deacons, Chancellors, Commissaries, Priests, Deacons or Halfpriests, Parsons, Viccars, Curats, Hireling roving Preachers, Church-wardens, Parish-clerkes: Also their Doctors, Proctors, and other officers of their spiritual courts (as they call them) together with the whole rable of the Prelates and their Servitours from and under them set over these Cathedrall and Parishionall Assemblies in this confusion are a strange and Antichristian ministerie and offices: and are not that ministerie above named, instituted in Christs Testament, nor placed in or over his Church.

Apoc, 9. 3. &c. and 13. 15. 16. 17. and 18. 15. 17. 2 Thes. 2. 3: 4. 8. 9. with Rom. 12. 7. 8. and with Eph. 11. 12. 1 Tim. 3. 15. and 5. 17. Let this Article be Confered with the preceden. 1. 7. 12. 13. 14. 19. 20. 21, 22, 23, 24, 28:

30 These their Popish offices, Entrance, Administration and mainten ance, with their names, titles, privileges, and prerogatives: also the power and rule they usurp over and in these Ecclesiasticall assemblies over the wholl ministerie, wholl ministration and affaires therof, yea one ouer another, creating Priests, citing, suspending, silencing, deposing, absoluing, excommunicating, etc. Their confounding of Ecclisiasticall and civile iurisdic-

tion, causes and proceedings in their persons, courts, commissions, visitations, the Priests of lesse rule, taking their ministery from and exercising it under them by their prescription ād limitation, swearing canonical obedience unto them, administring by their devised imposed, stinted popish Leitourgie, &c. Finally, the dispensations which they use for pluralitp of benefices, licences of non residency, licence to mary and eat flesh (both which with them are on certaine dayes ād tymes forbidden &c. These (we say) are sufficient proofs of the former assertion, the perticulars therin being duly examined by and compared to the rules of Christs Testamēt. Not to speake here, of Baptisme administred by midwives, of the Crosse used in Baptisme, of questions propounded to the infants, of the Priests surplice, prayer over the dead, at buriall, kneeling at the Lords supper, and other the like popish corruptions, almost infinite, reteyned and allowed among them.

Confer this article with the precedent 1.7.12.13 14,19.&c. also Revel.9.3.&c. and 13:11.15.16 17, and 14.9.10:11 and 17.3.4.5. and 18.15 17, and 22.18.19, Ioh.10,1. Luk. 22 25,26. Dan.7.8.25. and 8.10.11.12. 2 Thes.2:3.4.8.9.1 Pet 5:3. with Ioh.3.27.29, with Rev.2.1 1.Reg, 12; 27.&c. Zach.11.15.16. Esa.1.12 and 29,13 and 30.22 Mar.7.7.8 Gal. 1.8.&c. and 2.4.5, col.2.20.22,23,1 Tim.4.1.2,3. Ezec.8,5. and 13.9. &c. Mica.2 11 Mal.1,8 13.14.1 cor.14.34.35. Exo.20.4.5,6.7. Num.15 39 40 Psa,119.21.113.128. Deut 12.30—32.

31 These Ecclesiasticall Assemblies, remayning thus in, confusion and bondage under this Antichristian Ministerie Courts, Canons, worship, Ordinãces &c. without freedom and power to redresse anie enormitie among them, cannot be said in this confusion and subiectiō, truly to have Christ their Prophet Priest and King, neither can be in this estate, (whilest wee iudge them by the rules of Gods woord) esteemed the true, visible orderly gathered, or constituted Churches of Christ wherof the faithfull may become or stand Members, or have anie Spirituall communion with them in their publick worship and Administration.

confer this Article with the precedent : See also Reu, 18,2.3.4. 5. 1 cor.14,33. Ier.15.19. Mal,1 4.6.8 Hos.4.14.15. Rom,6.16 2 Pet.2 19 Lev.17.1---9.1 cor.10.14.17,18.19.20. 2 cor.6.14.15.16,17, Song.1.6,7.

32 Therfore are all that will be saved bound by Gods commādement with speed to come forth of this Antichristian estate, leaving the suppressiō of it: unto the Magistrate to whom it belōgeth. And all such also as have receyved or exercised anie of these false offices or anie pretended function or ministery in or to this false ād antichristiā constitutiō, are willingly in Gods feare to give over and leave those unlawfull offices, and no longer to minister in this maner to these assemblies in this estate.

Neyther may * any of what sort or condition soever, give any part of theirs Goods, Lands, Money, or money worth to the mainte nance of this false ministerie and worship upon any commandement or under anie colour whatsoever.

* Rev.18.4. Esa.48:20.& 52.11. Ier.50.8.& 51.6.45. Zach.2.6. 2 Cor.6.17. † Rev.17.16. Mat.22.21. 2 Chro.14.3.4.5.& 15.8.9. & 17.6. 2 King.23.5.&c. Rom.13.4.† Rev.18.4. Zach.13.2.4. 5.6.& 14.21. Ier.51.26. Psal.119.59.60.128. Prov.5.20. Esa.8. 11.12.& 35.8. "Rev.18.11. Prov.3.9.10. Psal.16.3.4.with Exod. 20.4.5. Iudg.17.3.4.5. Ezec.16.17.18.19. 1 Cor.10.19.20.21.22. with Heb.13.10. 1 Tim.5.17. 2 Cor.8.3.4.5.

33 And being come forth of this antichristian estate unto the freedom and true profession of Christ, besides the "instructing and well guyding of their owne families, they are willingly to ioyne † together in christian communion and orderly covenant, and by free confession of the faith and obediéce of Christ to unite themselves into † peculiar and visible congregations: wherin, as members of one body wherof Christ is the only head, they are to worship and serve God according to his word, remembring to * keep holy the Lords day.

"Gen 18.19. Exod.13.8.14. Pro.31:26.27. Eph.6.4:9, Deut.6. 7 Psal.78.3.4. † Luk.17.37. Phil.1.5. Ier,50.4.5, Act.2,41.42; Psal.110,3. Esa.44.5. Neh.9:38: 2 Cor.9:13.with † 1 Cor.1,2,& 12, 14.27.& 14.23,& 16,1, Act.14,23,27,& 15.3,4, & 16,5, Rom,12,5, Mat.18,17--20, Rev,1,20,& 2,1,8,12,18, & 3,1,7., 14, Eph,2.19. Col.2,19.* Exod,20,8.with Rev,1.10. Act.20.7, 1 Cor,16,2.

34. Then also * such to whom God hath given gifts to interpret the Scriptures, tryed in the exercise of Prophecy attending to studie and learning, may and ought (by the appointment of the congregation) to prophecy, according to the proportion of faith, and so to teach publickly the word of God, for the edification, exhortation and comfort of the Church: Untill such tyme as the people be meet for, and God manifest men with able guifts and fitnes to such Office or Offices as Christ hath appointed to the publick ministerie of his Church: But † no Sacraments to be administred untill the Pastors or Teachers be chosen and ordeined into theyr office.

* 1 Cor.14,chap. Rom,12,6, 1 Pet,4,10,11, 1 Cor,12.7. Act.13. 15, 1 Thes.5,20, † Heb.5.4. Eph,4.11,12. Num,16.10.39,40. Rom,12,7, Ioh.1,23.25, 1 Cor.1.14,15.16,17.with chap,3.5,6.

35 And

35 And then whereſoever ther ſhall be a people fit, and men furniſhed with meet and neceſſary guifts, they are not onely ſtill to continue the exerciſe of Prophecy aforſaid, but alſo upon due tryall to 'proceed unto choyce and ordination of Officers for the miniſtery ãd ſervice of the Church, according to the rule of Gods word: And ſo hold on ‡ ſtil to walke forward in the ways of Chriſt for theyr mutuall edification and confort, as it ſhall pleaſe God to give knowledge and grace thereunto. And particularly, that ſuch as be of the † ſeed, or under the governmẽt of anie of the Church, be even in their infancie receyved to Baptiſme, and made partakers of the ſigne of Gods covenant made with the Faithful and their ſeed throughout all generations. And that all "of the Church that are of yeares, and able to examine themſelves, doo communicate alſo in the Lords ſupper both men and women, and in *both kindes, bread and wine. In which ‡ elements, as alſo in the water of baptiſme, even after they are conſecrate, there is neyther tranſubſtantiation into, nor cõſubſtantiatiõ with the bodye and blood of Jeſus Chriſt: whom the heavens muſt conteyne, untill the tyme that al things be reſtored. But they are † in the ordinance of God ſignes and ſeales of Gods everlaſting covenant with us repreſenting and offring " to all the receyvers, but exhibiting only to the true beleevers the Lord Jeſus Chriſt and all his benefits unto righteouſnes, ſanctification, and eternall lyfe, through faith in his name to the glorie and prayſe of God.

* Aƈt.6,3.5,6.& 14. 21.22.23.Tit,1.5.&c. Eph.'4.11.12.1 Cor.12.7,8.14.15.28, 1 Tim.3.& 5,cap.Lev.8 cap. ‡col.2.5.6.7. 2.Theſ,2,15,Iud.ver,3.& Mat.28.20, † Aƈt. 2.38,39,with Rom.9.4.& Gen,17.7.12.27. Rom.11,16.1 Cor.1.16.& 7.14.& 10.2.Pſal.22 30. Col 2.11.12,Exod.12.48.49, Act.16.15.33,Mar.10.13.14.15,16, Gal.3.8.29. "Mat,26,26,27, 1 Cor.11.28,& 10.3,4,16.17,& 11,13.Act,2.42with.1,14,& 20.7.8,Gal.3,28. *Mat.26.26,27.1 Cor.10,3,4,16, et 11,23,24.25.26.27.28.29. ‡ 1 Cor.10,16,17.& 11.23 24,25,&c,Mat.26,26.27.29.& 15,17,Ioh,12.8, Act,3.21,&7.56, † Gen.17 11, Ronn,4,11,Exod.12,13with Heb,13.20, " 1 Cor.10,3,4,5,& 11,26,27.28,29,& 12.13,Rom,2,28,29,Col.2.11,12,13.Act,8,13,36,37.38,&15,9,Gal,3,27,Rom.5,& 6.& 7,& 8.cap. 1 Cor.1.30.31.

36 Thus being rightly gathered, eſtabliſhed, and ſtill proceeding in chriſtian communion and obedience of the Goſpell of Chriſt, none is to ſeparate for falts and corruptions, which may, and ſo long as the Church conſiſteth of mortall men, will fall out and ariſe among them, even in true conſtituted Churches, but by due order to ſeeke redreſſe therof.

Reu,2, &3,cap,Act,15,1,2,1,Cor,1,10,Phil,2,1—6&,3,15,16,Heb,10.25, Iudæ,ver,19,Leu,4,13,&c,2 Chron.15.9.17.&30,18,19, 2 Cor,13,1.2,1 Theſ. 5,14. 2 Theſ,3,6.14,Mat,18,17,1 Cor,5.4,5,

37. Such as yet ſee not the truth, may heare the publik doctine and prayers of the church, and with al meeknes are to bee ſought by all meanes: Yet none who are growne in yeares may bee received into

 their

their communion as members,‡ but such as doo make confession of their faith, publickly desiring to be received as members, and promissing to walke in the obedience of Christ. Neyther any infants,† but such as are the seed of the faithfull by one of the parents, or under their education and government. And further "not anie from one congregation to be received members in another, without bringing certificate of their former estate and present purpose.

* 1 cor.14.23,24.25.psa,18.49 Rom.15.9.10.1 Tim,2.4.2 Tim.2.25. ‡2cor.6,14:15.16.Ezra.4.3.Exod,12.43.Lev.22.25.Deut.7.cap.Exod.34.12 Esa.44.5.Psa.47.9and 110.3.Act 19.18.19.† Exod.20 5.6,1Cor.7 14: Ge.17 7.12.27, Exod.12,48.49 Act.16.15.33.Eph,4.4.5SeealsoArti.35.before"Act, 9.26.27 and 18.27.Rom.16.1.2.2 Cor.8.23.Col.4.10.

38 And although the particular congregations be thus distinct, and severall bodies, every one as a compact and knit citie in it self, yet are they all to walke by one and the same rule, and by all meanes convenient to have the counsell and help one of another in all needfull affaires of the Church, as members of one body in the common faith, under Christ their onely head.

Psal.122.3 cant.8.8.9 1 cor.4.17.and 16.1 Mat,28.20.1Tim.3.15.and 6 13 14Reu 22.18.19.col.2.6.19ãd4.16Act,15,cap.See besides the Article1.22,33

39 It is the office and dutie of Princes and Magistrates (who by the *ordinance of God are supreme governors under him over all persons and causes within their Realmes and dominions) to †suppresse and root out by their authoritie all false ministeries, voluntarie religions and counterfeit worship of God: to abolish and destroy the Idoll Temples: Images, Altars: Vestments, and all other monuments of idolatry and superstition: and to take and convert to their owne civile uses not only the benefit of all such idolatrous buildings and monuments: but also the Revenues / Demeanes / Lordships / Possessions / Gleabes and maintenance of any false ministeryes and unlawfull ecclesiasticall functions whatsoever within their dominions. And on the other hand to establish and mainteine by their lawes every part of Gods word / his Christian Religion / pure worship / and true ministery described in his word: to cherish and protect all such as are carefull to worship God according to his word / and to lead a godly lyfe in all peace and loyaltie: yea to enforce all their subiects whether ecclesiasticall or civile / to do their duties to God and men protecting and mainteining the good punishing and restraining the evill according as God hath commaunded / whose Lieutenants they are here on earth.

* Rom.13.1.2.. 1 pet. 2.13,14.2 chron. 19.4.&c and 29.and 34.cap.Iud.17 5.6.Mat.22.21,Tit.3.1. ‡ 2 Reg.23.5.&c Deu.12.2.3.with 17,14.18.19.20. 2 Reg.10.26.27.28, 2 chron,17.6,psa.101.pro.16.12.and 25.2,3.4,5,Act:19 27. Reu 17 16 and 18 11 12.&c. †Esa 49 23 and 60 3.10.11.12.Reu 21.24 Deu.17.14 18 19 20. psalm 2 10 11 12.and 72 1 &c and 101. Iosh. 1,7.8. 2 Chron 17 4.7 8.9 and 19.4 &c and 29.and 30 capit.Dan 6 25.26.Esra7. 26 pro 16 10 12. 13.and 20.28 and 29.14.Esa 10 1,2. 1 Tim.2 2. 1 pet.2 13 14. Rom.13.3 4.

40 And thus the protection and commandement of the Princes and

Magistrates maketh it much more *peaceable/ though no wit at all ‡more lawfull/ to walke in the wayes and ordinances of Jesus Christ which he hath commanded his Church to keep without spot and unrebukeable untill his appearing in the end of the world. And in this behalfe therefore the brethren thus mynded ād proceeding as is before said/ are both continually to †supplicate to God / and as they may/ to their Princes and Governours that thus and under them they may leade a quiet and peaceable lyfe in all godlines and honestie.

*Act.9.31 pro 16 15. Ezra 5 & 6. cap. 1Tim 2 2. Dan.6.25 26 Reu 21,24 ‡ Act 4,18 19 & 5 28.29. Dan.6-7.8,9,10.22. Luck 21,12.13. Mat 28,20 1Tim 5.21.& 6.13.14, †psal 20.9.&72.1.1 Tim.2,2.2chro. 15.1.2Hag. 1,1.4.14.&2.5

41 And if God encline the Magistrates hearts to the allowance and protection of the Church therin, it ought to be accompted a singular and happy blessing of God who granteth such nourcing Fathers and nourcing Mothers to his Church. And it behoveth all to be carefull to walke worthie so great a mercy of God in all thankfulnes and obedience.

psa. 126 1. Esa.49.23 ād 60.16. psal ,21&72. Rom.13.3 1Ti.m 22.3 4Act. 9.31

42 But if God withold the Magistrates allowance and furtherāce herein, yet *must wee notwithstanding proceed together in Christiā covenant and communion thus to walke in the obedience of Christ/ ād confessiō of his faith and Gospell even through the middest of all tryalls and afflictions / not accompting our goods / lands / wives / children / Fathers / Mothers / brethren / sisters / no nor our lyves dear unto us so as we may finish our course with ioy / remembring always that we ought to obey God rather then man: and grounding upon the ‡commandement / commission and promise of our Saviour Christ / who as hee hath all power in heaven and in earth / so hath also promised (if we keep his commandements which he hath given without limitation of tyme / place / Magistrates allowance or disallowance) to be with us unto the end of the world: and when we have finished our course and kept the faith/ to give us the crowne of righteousnes which is layd up for all that love his appearing

*Act.2.40.41.42.&4.19&5 28.29.41&16.20&c&17.6.7&20.23.24. 1Thes.3 3. phil.1.27.28.29 Dan,3.16.17.18.& 6.7.10.22.23,24 Luk.14.26:27.and 21.12 13.14. 2 Tim.2.12 and 3.12.Heb.10.32 &c 1 pet.4 cap. Reu.2.10.25.26 and 6. 9 and 12.11.17. ‡Mat,28.18.19.20.1 Tim.6.13.14.15.16. 2 Tim.4.7,8. Rev 2 10.and 14.12.13 and 22.16---20.

43 Unto all men is to be given whatsoever is due unto them. Tributes / Customes / and all other such lawfull and accustomed dutyes/ ought willingly and orderly to be payed and performed: Our lands / goods/ and bodyes / to be submitted in the Lord to the Magistrates pleasure. And the Magistrates themselves every way to be acknowledged / reverenced and obeyed according to godlines / not because of wrath only but also for conscience sake: And finally / all men so to be esteemed and regarded / as is due and meet for their place / age / estate and condition.

Rom.13.1.5.6.7.Mat.22.21.1 chron.27.cap.Ezra.7.26. Neh.9,36,37, tit.3 1.1 pe.2-13,&c,Exo18.12,20,12 &c Le,19,32,Iob,29.7 &c with 30,1 &c Eph,5 21--33& 6,1--9,1 pet,5-5,Tit,2-cap,

44 And thus, wee labour to give vnto God that which is Gods, and vnto Cesar that which is Cesars, and vnto all men, that which belongeth vnto them: Endevoring our selves to have alwayes a cleare conscience towards God and towards men: And having hope in God that the resurrection of the dead shalbe of the iust vnto life, and of the vniust vnto condemnation, everlasting.

Now if any take this to be heresie: then do wee with the Apostle freely confesse that after the way which they call heresie, wee worship God the Father of our Lord Jesus Christ: beleeving all things that are written in the Law, and in the Prophets and Apostles: And whatsoever is according to this rule of truth published by this State or holdẽ by anie reformed Churches in their Confessions abrode in the world. We do also reiect and detest all straunge and hereticall opinions and doctrines of all Hereticks both old and new whatsoever.

Mat, 22. 21, Act. 24. 14. 15. 16, Ioh, 5, 28, 29, Dan, 12, 2, 3. 2 Cor, 4, 17, 1 Tim, 6, 3. 4, 5. & 2 Tim. 1. 13, and 3, 14, 15, 16, 17,

45 Finally, wheras wee are much slandered and traduced as if wee denyed or misliked that forme of prayer commonly called the Lords prayer: wee thought it needfull here also concerning it to make known that we beleeve ãd acknowledg it to be a most absolute and most excellent forme of prayer, such as no men nor Angels can set downe the like. And that it was taught and appointed by our Lord Jesus Christ not that we should be tyed to the vse of those very words, but that we should according to that rule make all our requests and thanksgyving vnto God, forasmuch as it is a perfect forme and paterne conteining in it plaine and sufficient directions of prayer, for all occasions and necessities, that have ben, are, or shalbe, to the Church of God, or any member therof, to the end of the world.

Mat. 6, 9-13 Luk, 11, 2, 3, 4, with Mat, 14. 30 and 26, 39. 42, Ap, 1. 24, 25 and 4, 24, 30 and 6, 4, Rom, 8, 26, 27 and 15, 30, 31, 32, 1 Pet. 2, 5, Iam, 1, 5, 6 and 5. 13 1 Tim. 2, 1, 2. 3, Eph, 6, 18, 19, 1 Thess, 5. 17, 18, Phil, 4. 6, Reu, 8. 3. 4.

Now vnto him that is able to keep vs that wee fall not, and to present vs faltlesse before the presence of his glorie with ioy, that is, to God only wise our Saviour, be glory and maiestie, and dominion, & power, both now & for ever, Amen.

MAISTER IVNIVS HIS FIRST LETTER, CONCERNING THE CONFESSION OF FAITH AFORESAID.

To his beloved in Christ the Brethren of the English Church, now abiding at Amsterdam.

GRace mercie and peace from God the Father and our Saviour Iesus Christ. I have received of late (beloved Brethren in Christ) a little booke by one of your companie; which is intituled, *The confession of faith of some English men banished in Belgia*, and have knowne your desire partly by the speach of the same messenger, partly by the preface of the writing. But as concerning my selfe, beloved brethren, whom "for nearnes sake peradventure yee have thought meete to be called vpon apart, I verily see not how much I can doe in this cause, or how I can fit your purpose. For I knowe that now long since euery man doth abound in his owne sense; and that those that are other wise minded are "with a brotherly mynd so fare to be borne with, holding the heade and fundation, til the Lord reveale things further vnto them I know it is my part not to play the busie body, but that I should serve the truth and charitie in my standing and measure which the Lord hath bestowed vpon me, in Christian modestie and simplicitie, as farre as my skil and abilitie wil stretch vnto. Certainely when I considered" this cause more diligently, I thought nothing more commodious or more safe for the publick and for you and my selfe, in all this matter, the that we should embrace a holy silēce, if there be any thing, wherein we be offended, and that we commit our cause to the Lord, the author of our faith, and righter of our cause. But because after a sort, you will not suffer mee to be silent, and to cōdole in secret for the woundes of the Church, which is rent more then inough, by actions, especially being thrust forth in publik in this our age; I wil declare faith fully, and with a good cōscience before God what I thinke: beseeching him who is author of truth and peace that he would leade both you and me alike into all truth according to his promise, & also dispose each of our mindes and affections to interpret brotherly one anothers

M. Iunius his words are, propter vicinitatem which R. G. in his translation hath omitted.

Fraterno animo.

Causam hanc.

requestes, answeres, admonitions, and finally all our duties, although (as it commeth to passe, and is incident to man) disagreeing from our sense and taste.

I obserue therefore that there are three heads or chief poynts in your little booke, wherein you desire our counsell and iudgement The first head is of doctrine, which you professe in your little booke. The secōd is of fact, whereof yee accuse the English Churches. Lastly the third is, of the conclusion, which you inferre by comparing that your doctrine with that practise of England; namely that yee cannot with good conscience entertaine a communiō with those Churches, but that yee doe abhorre them with all your heartes. Therefore I will speak briefely of

Vt sentio. these 3. things," what I think, entreating you brotherly to take my answere in good part.

I marvell that the point of doctrine, or little booke of your confession, beloved brethrē, is sent ouer to me. I marvell that it was sent ouer to all the students of holy Scriptures in all Christian Vniuersities; for if there be a certaine consent of doctrine as you pretend it, truely I do not see what need there was, that you should set forth a newe confession in this consent of holy and auncient doctrine. But if there be a dissention peradventure in the doctrine, or rather a differēce, that in deed ought not to bee dissembled, if so be that yee thought it necessarie, that your doctrine should be declared.

Besides, in that you send to mee; yea that you send to publicke viewe,

Confessionem. " your confession, I marvell, brethren, yea I greatly maruell, what your meaning should bee, both in respect of the ende and the fact For if ye haue set it foorth to that end, that yee might purge your selues, I pray you brethren, wherefore doe yee desire, to purge your selues with so many soules; who have not knowē you as yet to bee accused; who can neuer take knowledge of the right or wrong of your accusation; and who are not called vnto it by any lawfull means? and (that which is worse) wherfore would yee haue this done before so many " deadly e-

Infestis. nemies to God and the Church, who thirst after nothing so much as the blood of the Church of God, and doe rejoyce that we vndiscreetly make a publishing of these wounds: that they by these very wounds might spoyle the Church, that pretious bodie of Christ, of the blood of veritie, and juyce of charitie? Finally, why doe yee this before so many weake ones, who not yet knowing, that yee are borne (as I may so say) are offēded, rather with a carcasselike stink of schismes in the Church, before they knowe certainely the bodie whereunto they may cleaue?

Alas

Alas brethren, is your purgation so much worth vnto you that therfore the publicke good of the Church should bee brought into so greate danger? A Christian an humble, and godly minde ought to bee otherwise affected, and setting aside the respect of their owne priuate good, constantly thus to determine, let the earth rather first swallowe me vp (as the Poet saith) and let mee rather bee accursed for my brethren, then that by me, and for my credit sake even one of these little ones should be offended and kept from comming to Christ, and abiding in Christ my Sauiour. Verily let what will of my estimation goe to wracke, who am a Christian, let me be trampled vnder all mẽs feete, so that by my fact, I take nothing from Christ, from his body, no not the lest thing." And that you my brethren are thus determined and resolved bending all your counsels to this end; I am as strõgly perswaded, as he that is most. But the end which you have in common, alas for griefe, in this particular case (pardon if I speake more freely, for yee would have me to speak) from it yee seeme to have erred. For herein, if I see anie thing, the contemplation of your cause hath deceyved you, which thing I trust yee your selves without doubt will marke if ye would goe a little from that your particular sense "from your cause.

Atque hoc quidẽ fratres vobis esse constitutum deliberatũq. huc adlaborare consilia vestra, tã sum persuasus, &c.

Sed quem finem in communi habetis, at eo &c. videmini aberrasse.

A causa vestra.

I have shewed that there is some errour in that end. Let vs come to the fact. In the fact yee frame a purgation of your selues. That thing is denyed to none, if there be cause, if measure, if place, if time. But wherefore with mee brethren, who doe neither heare these accusations of yours; neither if I should heare them, would I receive them rashly? Wherefore in publick? where yee knowe that it falleth out for the most part, that they who purge them selues, before they be accused, eyther bewray thẽselues, or raise suspiciõs against themselues more easely thẽ they can afterward wash away. Yee knowe that the publicke voice is neither a iust iudge oftentimes, nor at any time almost a lawfull Iudge; so greatly doth evil preuaile and beare sway in the publick. Therefor yee appeale to these Iudges, who can neither iudge, not take knowledge: finally, they are not onely no Iudges, but not so much as witnesses: so the private cause is not furthered, and the publique is many waies hindered. Ye will say thẽ, who shall bee? What judges, what witnesses shal we call vpon? Your owne preface shall answere yee for me. For whẽ, ye pronũce that ye have foũd a place of rest by the mercy of God in these places (ye doe acknowledge I thinke your owne words) ye plainely signifie two things. One, that if ye have found a place of rest, ye shall doe wisely, if ye doe not stirre, where ye may be in quiet. The other that where you haue a lodging, and a quiet seate that there in deed you must receiue the iudgement of your doctrine and faith, if ye will have the same lawfully knowne and approoued. Ye are in a Church furnished with the seruants of God, whose pietie. learning, and brotherly loue to the members of Christ good men doe know. It is an vnlawfull course verily, to omit those among whom yee are and to call upon another Church, or the whole publik state," or this Vniversity, or me who am a weake member therein, either in part, or in common. This order is godly, iust, lawfull, and tendeth to peace, and edification, which you ought first, modestly to have regarded, and to which I being a weake brother, am bounden by brotherly duetie, to recall my brethren, that goe astray, and not to be caried headlong, and to rush vpon the knowledge of things by this meanes offred; besides all equitie and good order. Till ye shall doe this, I admonish, exhort, pray, and beseech by the most sacred & holy name of Christ, that ye would not call vpon me, neither any other, neither the publick it self: for by this preposterous course (as we may so say) ye do not disburthen your selues, as ye thinke, of enuy and blame (if there be any) but ye doe with suspition and præjudice burthen your owne cause," which I verily do not preiudice at all, I speak it religiously before the Lord. Let them speake first, with whom yee soiourne, whom yee deny not to be your brethren But if peraduenture they shall not satisfie you, or yee shall not satisfie them, then let a new course be taken by lawfull order. This no good man will denie, but till this be attempted, it will be vnprofitable to you, and hurtfull to the Church, to take another course. But neither I, nor my Colleagues, nor other wise men, will euer be so vnwise as to preuēt or take this thing out of the hands of them, to whom the knowledge thereof doth of right appertaine. And so much of the doctrine.

Aut Academiam hanc.

Cui ego quidē nullū præjudiciū facio, religiose dico coram Domino.

I come to the accusation which yee use against the Church of England, as ye write. In this accusation beloued brethren, I doe louingly entreat you, that yee would not take it in ill part, if I doe admonish yee of a few things which I thinke, I may of right doe. First, what need is there, that yee should accuse them? Yee haue giuen place, yee haue (as wee may so speake) passed ouer into another Court: Wherefore you haue giuen place, no body desireth to know, or doth trouble you. If wrong be done you in England (that I may grant there was done: it belongeth not to me, to affirme or deny who haue not knowne it) yet this iniury hath ceased to prosequute you being departed from them. What compelleth you to be mooued, and to take vpon you, the burthen

Vt dem fuisse factā.

then of accusation? Why are yee not quiet being without the daunger of any hurt? Why doe yee not rather passe ouer the iniury that is past? Why doe yee not beare it (if there be yet any) in silence and hope, rather then to mooue that which is in rest? It is plainely a Christian part, if thou beare it, and a prudent part, if thou abstaine from stirring the euill that is well appeased, an impotent thing, if thou doe contrariwise. Impotens.

And to what end I pray you is it? To the end that you might purge your selues? But here is no man that doth repeate anew, or lay these accusations against you. Wherefore serueth this purgatiō? that yee may be euen with them against whom yee cōplaine? But this is not the part of a Christian. I doe not thinke that this is your meaning. Is it to reforme them? This indeed is an holy endeuour. But if yee could not doe this when yee were present, cōsider what yee can doe when yee are absent. But first of all consider with your selues, by what meanes yee take this way, namely to accuse to me, to others, to the publike, in the theatre of the Church, in the circle of the world. Ah beloued brethren, was it euer heard of, that any priuate man (to say nothing of a great communitie) was euer amended by this course Further consider I pray you before whom yee bring these things. I will speak of my selfe, to whom alone yee would commit this your little booke; I know not whether in this your little booke yee call upon me, as an intercessor, or examiner, or a Iudge. For if as an intercessor, were it not better that your cōplaints were kept secret, then layed open (which tendeth to reproch) and the Church of Christ, innumerable soules, weake, strangers, to be beaten with the types of your impression. It is most manifest, that they against whom yee deale, wil be more prouoked "by this grieuous sting. If as an examiner, by what right can I doe it? who haue no lawful authority from God, from the Church, from the Magistrate, or frō both the parties: neither if it should be committed, would I easily accept it; I am so priuie to my selfe, of my owne insufficiencie; for who am I? or what am I? that I should be able, throughly to see euery particular thing, concerning you, and them, which are required to a iust examination. And this the right course of examination doth require, otherwise (as *Seneca* wisely saith) he that judgeth one party being not heard, albeit he iudgeth that which is right, yet he is vniust. Yee are not a little deceiued in this your iudgement beloued brethren: Yee almost do me an iniury, when ye call me to be a busie body, or think that I wil take upon me the part of an examiner, or (that which is more subject to envie and farre from duetie) of a Iudge And brethrē, that which I say of my selfe,

Hoc gravi aculeo.

 thinke

Qui vbiuis locorum sunt. thinke that is the answere of the other brethren" which are any where els in Churches and Vniversities. No wise man will rashly goe downe these steps, or clime vp to this seate of judgement. In deed concerning your faith and doctrine something may be said, if you expound it, and if the thing be done in order. But touching the accusatiō of your coūtreymen and of matters passed to and fro; no wise man by my consent, Hac lege. wil, on this condition take vpon him the burthen of iudging.

And for Gods sake, consider the event of this fact. For I pray you whom would it profit if that were done which yee desire? Certainly neither would it profit you nor thē, nor these with whom ye soiourne, nor the Church of God. Contrariwise whom would it not hurt? This thing would set you more on fire:" as contentions are woont the more to make hote, the more they are stirred. It would more alienate them whom yee pretend to be to injuriously enstranged from you: For this is not the way of teaching, nor of informing, nor of seeking reconciliation. It would rent asunder the good men whose hospitality yee doe now commodiously vse either frō you, or amongst themselues (which duetie they have not deserved of you by their hospitalitie,) It would set a more grievous fier on the whole Church, and spread through all her ioynts, which God turne away And that" vnwise mā which should vsurpe this authority, it would make a scorne to ill tōgues, while good men would pittie his vaine labour and your expectation. Lastly (that I may also adde this, and marke brethren, how sincerely and brotherly I deale with you) albeit I might and would lawfully give sentence both of your faith which yee declare, and also of the fact of accusatiō which yee bend against your countreymen: Yet yee by this course and maner of dealing have taken from me the authority of doing that which yee require touching your fact; your selves by this maner of request do hinder your owne desier. Ye will marvalle perhaps at that which I say, and yet it is so. For you doe so require my iudgement as you doe also with all require the iudgement of all Vniversities and Students. If you request this in common; then you doe not desire that I should doe it alone: but if particularly, doe you thinke that any of vs will be so mad, that when the judgement of so many good men and diligence is desired, some one *Palæmon* should take vpon him the chiefest parts: and should by him selfe speake of that thing, which is required of so many as learned, yea better learned, and better furnished with pietie, judgement, and experience, which requireth a serious consultation, an holy communication, and a ripe inoffensive judgment.

Res ista vos magis inflammaret, prout contentiones magis fervefacere solent quò moventur magis. Illos magis abalienaret, quos iniquius abalienatos à vobis esse obtenditis, &c.

Imprudentem.

But

But now of the third thing what shal I say?" your selves I think, beloved brethren, do mynd that if I cannot on this condition, neyther ought, to give answer concerning the two points aforesaid, it would be vtterly vnjust if I should as yet determine any thing on eyther side towching the cōclusion which you draw frō thence, that is, from those premisses. But I verily suspēd my iudgemēt, brethrē I suspend my iudgemēt in this cause, even as God & nature, & reason, and al lawes command me to do. Ye know I think the causes by these things which ye haue now read, & shal learne besides by other things which God shal minister vnto you (I hope) by the spirit of trueth and wisdome. I ought not to iudge with my selfe of matters vnknowne, at least not so evident, neither yet with such forward boldnesse to pronoūce among you or others, the matter being not sufficiently manifest to my selfe. God knoweth and iudgeth," to whom stand or fall as many as are his servants. Otherwise I trust yee are not ignorāt that there are three things which euē frō the verie infancie of the Church, the holy fathers would haue to be distinguished by the word of God, among the people of God, namely, faith or doctrine, conversation or manners, and the order of discipline. And all wise men haue taught this with one consent, and delivered it to posteritie, that where the foundation of the truth of doctrine remaineth, which is the piller of saluation, although with most corrupt manners and discipline, there the Church remaineth, & that no man ought rashly to separate himselfe from that Church (whiles he may tarry in it without ship wracke of faith and conscience) or take from it the name of a Church, especially seeing euery Church consisteth of Pastors and flocke, which if some Pastors or Prelates trouble, yet it is vnmeete that this name either should be taken away from the other Pastors, which Christ doth witnesse by the doctrine of truth, or from the flocke which Christ hath purchased with his owne bloode, and doth daily sanctifie with the washing of the newe birth by the worde. This ought to be sufficient for you if any thing have offended you at home, that now the fatherly & mercifull providence of God hath provided for you elsewhere. Certainely whiles yee inueigh against those Churches, yee shal make that your cause neuer the better, neither more probable with good men: which thing if yee have not yet considered and conceived by my aduise and counsell, and by the admonition of those which wish you wel, experience it selfe at last (God grant it be not to late, and he informe you in good) will prooue all these things vnto you. For by the trueth of doctrine, holinesse of life, by the worke of faith and patience, and by the dueties of charitie euen towards them of whome yee professe that ye are wronged, yee shal rather approove your selves and your cause, thē by outcryes and publishing of writings, euen as our Sauiour is saide to bring iudgement to victorie not by filling the streetes with shouting and clamours, but by blowing gently into the smoking flax and tender handling the bruised reede.

Which thinges seeing they be so, I beseech you most louing brethrē in Christ by that most holi name of Christ which ye professe, by those bowels of mercie,

Ipsi opinor, fratres charissimi, animadvertitis, si de antecedentibus illis duobus capitibus nec possum ea lege, nec debeo respōsum dare, id planè iniquū fore si de ea conclusione, &c.

Cui stant.

quòd jam, &c.

mercie, wherewith Christ hath embraced vs frō on high, that yee would thinke of another course, that yee would take another way to salvation, to edificatiō, to peace." If there be consent, shake not your faith, which is not to be winnowed againe by new reasons, This course is suspitious. But if it must needs be sifted, let it suffice you that it be first approved by those servants of God among whome yee dwell: this is certainnly a lawfull course: Forgiue the former iniuries if any have beene, by Christian charitie to them from whom yee have received the same, & hide them frō others by Christiā wisdome. There is no feare, that by so doing yee should " be burst: God will enlarge your harts by the spirite of charitie most cōmodiously. Looke to your selues that overcomming al sharpnesse and al bitternesse of minde yee may be acceptable to Christ and profitable to the Church, and that " the sweet odour of your pietie may be spread in speach, in life, in order to all the godly without the stench of enmitie and schisme. Iudge not that yee be not iudged: But abstaine from those heavie determinations and conclusions (as they call them) against othermen, neither labour either to get Abetters or partakers in that your former iudgement (which would be falde in you to be a spice of faction in them of imprudencie, or else to drawe them to an vnseasonable, vncivill, inconvenient and dangerous deliuerie of opinions. Pitie your selues I beseech you (most louing brethren) and the whole flocke which is gathered among you. Haue pittie of them whome thorough error & infirmitie yee cry out be hurt. Pitie your entertainers among whome it were a most iniurious thing that ye should sowe these tares, especially being admonished. And it would be a greate indignitie by clamours and writings to brede in them suspicions and finister opinions, eyther of your selves or of those your adversaries (as you count them) or els of both. Finally pitie the Church of Christ, which verily it is not comely, nor expedient neither in any case tolerable amōg so many and greeuous wounds which are " universally given vnto it, to be further galled with this particular wound: So let God almightie loue you and Iesus Christ that most mercifull Lord, and our Sauiour be mercifull vnto you. And if I shall be able to doe any good in the publicke cause and yours, assure your selves that I will spare no diligence, no labour, no paines, that you with vs and all togither may be filled with sāctimony (without which none shal se God) with the good things of the Lord in his house, and before his face. And the God of peace which hath raised from the dead our Lord Iesus that great sheepeheard of the sheepe, by the blood of the eternall couenant, make you perfect in euery good worke to doe his will, working in you, that which is acceptable in his sight by Iesus Christ, to whom be glorie for ever and ever, Amen. And I pray you brethren suffer this word of exhortation, which I have briefely writte vnto you. The grace of God be with you all, Amen. From Leyden this Saturday the 9. of Ianuary. 1599.

Si consensio est.

Rumpamini.

Odor suavissimus.

Vniverse. vniversally, or, every where.

Yours in the Lord Francis Iunius.

The answer to the Letter aforesaid.

To the Reverend and learned Mr. Francis Iunius, our beloved brother in Christ, At Leyden in Holland.

GRace and peace from God the Father and the Lord Iesus Christ our Saviour. Reverend Sr. and beloved brother in Christ, we have lately received your letter, which you sent unsealed to the Ministers of the Dutch and french Churches, that it might first be read of thē, and them be delyvered to us. We have also read and weighed it, and thougt it meet to wryte agayne, partly to thank you that vouched safe to write unto us: partly to satisfy you (if we can) in some thinges wherein we see you are mistaken: In the wryting wherof, we humbly request that speaking freely that which the thing it self requireth you would take it in good part, as you are woōt. Many thinges indeed you have wrytten which we do willingly acknowledg and consent therein with you. Those we will not touch at all. The rest we will prosequute in the same order, as by your self they are propounded.

Whereas there was a litle booke exhibited unto you by one of us, it is not so to be takē, as if you were called upō alone or apart from others. For the brother which delyvered you the booke certified us, that this passed betwene you, that by you it should be communicated with your Colleagues the governours of that University, and that you tooke upon you to do it. Now if you have so done, how is it that you alone wryte back againe? why also do you so often repeat and seeme to reprehend that you, you (we say) alone, apart, are called upon? If you have not done it, mynde then on whome the blame lyeth that it is not communicated with thē in that University, to whome by us it was dedicated. And we do now agayne entreat you, that being myndfull of your promyse you would performe it: that so you with the other learned and godly men and brethren there, may eyther convynce our fayth and cause of errour, or els together with us conted for this fayth once gyven to the Saints. The one of these we take it must needes be donne. And we gather it by comparing together Iam. 5.19.12. with Iude ver. 3. This also is the very thing which we did desire and still do desire in that Epistle dedicatory. And let these thinges once spoken, suffyce (we pray you) for the crimination of calling on you apart, which in this letter of yours you have so oftē objected and repeated.

Next you propound three tinges to be considered in the booke it self, of which you promyse to speake, briefly and brotherly, what you thinke.

1. The first head (you say) is of the doctrine, which we professe in our booke. Be it so indeed. Here we expected (because you purpose to wryte of the doctrine we professe) that you would have discussed the articles of our fayth, and reproved the errours (if there be any) by the light of Gods word. And who would not have expected this? But behold, there is not a word of the doctrine and fayth it self. What may this meane? Is it because your self beleeu this faith to be trew, sound groūded on the word of God and agreable therunto? If so, why thē wryting these thinges, do you not professe it? Why do you dissemble it? specially, whē you heare that this fayth is traduced as schisme, as heresy? but you see perhaps that in the doctrine of faith we erre from the truth. If it be so, why then wryte you, and yet shew not the errours? why do you not (as much as in you is) bring into the way such as do erre? No not whē request is made that the errours may be shewed by the light of the holy Scripture? Certainly your godlynes perswadeth otherwise: yea, God himself requireth otherwise. Iam. 5.19.20.

F Yet now

Yet now when you touch not the doctrine it self, what is it that you wryte in this behalf? Even this only, that you would perswade we have erred herein that we have publyshed the confession of our faith. First of al this concerneth the maner, not the matter it self. But yet let us weigh your reasons: If (say you) there be a certayne consent of doctrine: then there was no need that we should set forth a new Confession in this agreement of holy and ancient doctrine. Doe you indeed speak as you thinke? How is it then that some while synce, when the Germane and French Churches had before publyshed their Confessions of fayth, yet afterward the Belgick, Scotish, and other Churches set forth theirs also, notwitstanding that they agreed with them in the holy and annicient doctrine? Yea tell us (we pray you) what you think of that godly and learned Mr. Beza his pryvate Confession of fayth lately publyshed? Not to speake of many other wrytten and divulged by many of the martyrs also, in their severall ages. Do not all these agree in the holy and annyent doctrine of Godlynes? Or should not therfore these Confessions have bene publyshed? What soever you shall say for them, mynd the same also as spoken for us. Secondly you say, if there be any dissention in doctrine, that ought not to be dissembled, &c. But what is this to us, who have playnely shewed and reckned up the thinges wherein we dissent from the Church of England, with whom we have to do in this behalf? Neyther that only, but have also in our Confession not obscurely signified, concerning the thinges wherein the other Churches of this city and ours as yet do not agree.

After these thinges, you come to discusse the end and fact of our publyshing this Confession. Touching the end, we have shewed it in the epistle and preface set before the booke it self. And we answer further, that we did this to the same end, that all the reformed Churches of late did publysh theirs. For proof whereof, let the preface of the Harmony of Confessions, compared with ours, speak for us. If you take away the reasons by both alleadged, we yeeld. But if you cannot, then see whether both here and other where often in this letter you do not through our sydes strike at all these Churches lykewise. Our cause and cleering, we commyt to God and to all godly that love the truth. Such as before knewe not our cause they may now by this meanes have knowledge therof. Such as be enemyes of God, of the Church, of the truth, have nothing by this book of ours, whereof to rejoyce. They will rather be grieved when thus they shall see Antichrist that man of synne to be more and more discovered, whom the Lord in the end will wholy consume and abolysh, with the spirit of his mouth in the testimony (not in the silence) of his servants. 2. Thes. 2.8. with Rev. 12.11. and 14.6.7.8. and 20.4. Fynally, such as be weak and by reason of the stink of schismes know not the true body of Christ whereunto they should joyne themselves, they may by this meanes be better instructed and induced more certainly to know and imbrace the true Church and fayth of Christ. Thus desyre we that the publyck good of the Church be holpe forward, that Christ may have the preeminence over all. And thus have we spoken of the end, in which as yet we see not any mistaking or errour.

Touching the fact, we answer in lyke maner as before concerning the end. Yea and the thinges which here you bring, for not doing it in publyck, you may urge the very same lykewise against all the reformed Churches, against Athanasius, Origen, Augustine, Tertullian, and others of the fathers, against Zuinglius, Luther, Calvine, Beza, and many other of these ages, godly men, and divers of them

them also Martyrs of Jesus Christ: who have set forth in publyck their Confessions of fayth private their apologies/complaynts/disputations/yea and their letters concerning matters in religion publyckly controverted. But these things perhaps came not in your mynd/ whiles there was before your eyes only the contemplation of our particular cause: which thing your self (we trust) will perceive/ if you turne your eyes a lytle from us unto others approved by your self. Moreover howsoever the evill (whereof you wryte) do prevayle in publyck: yet alwayes and every where wisdome is justified of her children/ as Christ hath taught Mat. 11. 16. 19. And this shall suffice us and all that are godly Lastly/ in a case of such weight and necessity/ who should rather be called upon then the students of the holy Scriptures in Christian universityes? Who (we pray you) are esteemed to be of better or sounder judgment? Whome doth it more concerne to take knowledg/ of the truth and errours in religion? Who should better instruct in the truth/ or convince falshood? And to conclude/ who can or ought to attend more to the discussing of these things?

But you object/ that seeing we have here found place of rest, here also we must receive the judgment of our doctrine and fayth, if we will have the same lawfully knowen and approved, &c. Here come many things to be considered. First what if the rest and breathing/ which here we enjoye/ come unto us/ not by the Ministers (of whome you speak) but by the Magistrats: which we do alwayes and every where acknowledg with thanckes. Secondly what if these ministers (men indeed learned and wise) should be of the same mynd with you/ that they would not heare or speake any thing concerning our fayth and cause: inasmuch as they would not be eyther intercessours, or examiners, or Iudges? Furthermore/ what if our Confession of fayth have ben exhibited to them above three yeares synce/ that by them it might eyther be approved/ or the errours (if there be any) convinced? What if some of them have denounced us as hereticks and schismaticks? What if they have received certayne articles full of lyes and sclaunders/ spread abroad against us/ and yet to this daye have not gyven us a copy of them/ no though they were desyred? What if upon occasion offered we have dealt with them touching certaine corruptions yet remayning in their Churches/ which notwithstanding they would not so much as acknowledg? And finally/ what if we after the concealing and not regarding of all these thinges/ have now agayne this last yeare delyvered them the Confession of our fayth in wryting/ before it was put forth in print? You see what we could answer in this behalf: but we would rather have buryed these thinges in forgetfulnes/ if you had not so urged us as from you they might not now be concealed. Pardon you therfore and let them also (we intreat) pardon us/ that we speak freely: for you would have us speak/ yea you constreyne us against our will to wryte these things/ which we would have covered in silence/ hoping hereafter for better. Besydes these/ we answer also that in the preface before our Confession is signified/ that not here only but almost every where we are traduced as heretickes/ and schismaticks: and that therfore it concerned us/ to declare our fayth and cause not to these only but unto all. The very thing which before us on lyke occasion (as is aforesaid) both dyvers of the ffathers have don of old/ and in later tymes almost all the reformed Churches and of the Martyrs not a few.

And hitherto of your reasons alleadged against the publyshing of our

our fayth: Which how weak they are/now judg your self. But suppose they were strong/ and that therfore herein we had erred/that our Confession came forth in publyck: yet now it is publyshed the errours (if any be found in it) are certeynly to be shewed and convinced by the word of God.

Otherwise you may easily gather that we shall be more cōfirmed in this fayth. And seing you (Learned Sr.) do purposely wryte cōcerning the Doctrine which we professe/ and yet shew not any one errour in the Doctrine: consider wel what you have done. Will you be ready to help them who erre (as you think) in the manner and circumstāces? and will you afford no help at all in the matter and fayth it self? Far be this from you from your godlynes/learning/wisdome/charity. And thus much of the first poynt/which you noted concerning doctrine.

2 The second head is of the fact wherof (as you say) we accuse the Englysh Churches. Here also we expected/ that you would have discussed those fower poynts/ which are particularly rehearsed in the preface of this book/and which we shewed to be done and used by them dayly in their divine worship: for which also we testifyed that we are banished and have departed from them. But of these neyther/have you not one word And yet this was the specyall fact/ which we noted for to be considered in that Church. That other of the Prelats tyranny and persecution of vs/we touched but by the way and in a few wordes. We marvell therfore/ yea and greatly marvell that these thinges which directly concerne the matter and cause it self/should thus every where be let passe by you/who yet pretend to bring into the way such as do erre. But les vs see nevertheles what the thinges are/which you do here so much vrge.

The first is/that those Churches from which we have departed, should not by vs be accused. About the word accusation we will not contend: Onely this we say/ we vse it not (that we remember) except whē we treat of our owne cause who by them are accused of heresy Schisme sedition etc. Of which forasmuch as we are accused among them/ here and every where: what good man will deny vnto vs place of defence: But you say/no man desyreth to know why we came thence, and that the injury also hath left to prosequute vs being departed from them How these things escaped you/we marvell. For in both of them you wryte otherwise then the thing is. For both many do dayly desier to know why we came thence/ and the injury hath prosequuted vs being departed/into this place to this very day. Of the former we need cyte no witnesses: for they are almost infinite. Of the latter/ besydes the Latine bookes publyshed at home by our owne contreymen/ besydes the libels which they have sparsed against vs in this city besydes the sclaunders wherewith they do also pursue vs every where: besydes all these (we say) the Ministers them selves of the Churches Dutch and Frēch both here at Amsterdam and at Dordrecht are able to testifye. they have received (as we said afore) certeyne articles full of lyes and sclaunders/wrytten against vs/and yet still they have them for ought we know. Moreover/if none of these things had fallē out opēly before the world/yet who knoweth not that Antichrists retinew (such as be the Prelats) do still resemble the nature and conditions of the Dragon/ who out of his mouth cast waters like a flood after the woman/ that he might cause her to be caryed away of the flood/whom being present he could not devoure Rev. 12. and 13 chap.

As for that you annexe of concealing injuryes, it hath ben observed by vs/ as much as we could. For neyther have we in particular related them/ neyther can we/if we would. We have noted only in generall/ that these Prelats have done the very things/ which the Scripture foretold should by the Beast and Antichrist be commytted Neyther are we in this kind of wryting/eyther the first/or alone. Thus heretofore have many of the servants of God wrytten/ who in their severall countries have ben many wayes vexed by Antichrist. Neyther that only/ but they have also noted downe the particuler persons/ names/ places/ tymes/

martyr-

martyrdomes/causes/actions/injuryes. Search (if you please) the ecclesiasticall writers almost of every age: search the Acts and momments of the martyrs / in this countrey in ours/in Scotland/in France / in the other countryes almost all here about: yea search the Acts of the Apostles/ and see if such particular historyes be not there also recorded. Yet further/tell vs (we pray you) if this course had ben held by all/ which you seem to exact of vs ? from whence then could you or any other have that knowledg and evidence/ as now is had / of the fulfilling (throughout severall ages/of those prophecyes which are in the Scriptures/of the Beast/ of the false Prophet/of Antichrist/of his mysterey/exaltation/tyranny/marchants discovery/fall/etc. How should from their owne Acts / the adversaryes mouthes be so stopped/as now we see/heare/ and read / is dayly done by the martyrs and servants of Christ? Lastly/how could your self and other learned men have so expounded that divine book of the Revelation (not to speak of other Scriptures lykewise interpreted) as you have now already done/which great fruit/and gratulation of all the godly?

Of the end which here againe you urge/we have spoken both before in this letter/and in the epistles prefixed to the book it self. Adde hereunto/ that if the Prelats and other adversaryes of the truth be not by these and the lyke wrytinges amended/they shall yet doubtlesse be made the more unexcuseable. The visard also/by which they have deceyved you (as it seemeth) and almost all others/was to be pulled of. But this could not be donne for the knowledg of all (as was meet) otherwise then by publick wryting. To omytt others/we appeale unto your conscience (learned S.) whether you did think the estate of that Church and of those Prelats to be such in any measure touching their Antichristian constitution / leitourgy/ministery/Hierarchy (which your self acknowledg to be that other beast/ in Rev. 13, 11. 18.) as now for certeyne you heare and see it in that book as it were paynted out before your eyes. But of these things phough is sayd in the book it self. Surely these and the lyke their unfruitfull workes of darknes/ were to be re- Eph. 5. 11. prooved/not dissembled/not allowed: especyally seing they are so stiffely by them Rev. 18. 6. 7 retayned/defended/urged: and that under a pretence of the Gospell / with which Jer. 50. 14. they have no more agreement then darknes hath with light/ Beliall with Christ. Neyther is this to take up burthens of Accusations, but to take away the visard of Antichristian apostasy / and to witnes the truth of Jesus Christ against Antichrist. which duty our Lord and Saviour Christ requireth of you / of vs / of all the godly: the Lord (we say) who in these latter tymes hath begunne to discover that lawles man of sinne / and will at length consume him with the spirit of his mouth/by the word of the testimony of his servants. So far of is it that they should be accounted busy bodyes, which performe this duty to Christ: or that we herein have don you any iniury. So far of also is it/that we should think what you speak of your self, the same to be answered vs by the rest of the bretheren that are any where els in Churches, in Vniversityes. Not to speak of others we know that Mr. Beza that worthy servant of God hath in causes not much unlyke answered otherwise. But of this matter more herafter. In the meane tyme (that we also may deale syncerely and brotherly with you) mynd we pray you / whether you have not done your self iniury/whiles you have climed into this seate/so confidently to pronounce that of others wherof (as we think) you cannot any way have certaine knowledg; yea whiles you alone determyne of that matter/ which (to use your owne wordes) requireth serious consultation and holy communication.

Couching the event, we commit it to God/who (we certeynly hope) will worck al these things for good both to vs/and to the by whom we are exiled/and to these amonge whom we sojorne/and to the Church of God every where. And to whom (we pray you) would it not be good / if that were done / which we desier? For our

F 3 selves,

ſelves, if we erre/ let the righteous ſmyte and reprove vs/ it ſhalbe a benefyt and precious oyntment unto vs. For our adverſaries, if they be the more eſtraunged/ it ſhalbe their owne fault/not ours/ nor theirs that ſhall godlyly and freely teſtifie what they ſee in this cauſe: And who knoweth/ whether by this meanes they may be brought to conſider more then heretofore both of the unlawfull conſtitution of that Church/ and of their outragious crueltye: and thereupon ſeriouſly endevour a godly redreſſing of the former/ and an utter repreſſing of the latter? For the good among whom we ſojourne, they ſhall have better knowledg of our fayth and cauſe: they may alſo grow vp together more ſtrongly in the truth of the Goſpell/ whiles thus they are ſtirred vp more carefully to endevour that the corruptions wherewith their Churches yet are faulty may be duly abolyſhed/ and whiles ſuch as are ſeduced by the errours of the Papiſts/ Anabaptiſts/ and other heretickes troubling theſe Churches/ are upon this occaſion drawne from ſuch eſtate and ſtirred vp to ſearch/ knowe/ and embrace the truth of the Goſpell. Fynally for the whole Church, we hope that it ſhall hence alſo receive much profyt/ if this fayth and cauſe (which now a long tyme hath ben condemned for ſchiſme and hereſy) if alſo that Antichriſtian Apoſtaſy (which now a long tyme under the viſard of godlynes hath deceived the world in the myſtery of iniquity) if theſe things we ſay/ being of ſo great moment/ be examyned and diſcuſſed by the canon of the Scriptures/ of ſo many and ſo worthy men furnyſhed with learning/ godlynes/ judgment/ wiſdome. And thus much of the ſecond poynt/ which was concerning the fact.

The third (you ſay) is of the concluſion inferred upon comparing together the doctrine and fact aforeſaid. Here firſt you affirme/ you with-hould your ſelf in ſuſpence in this cauſe. Be it ſo. It is God that can reveale this alſo unto you/ and perſwade your conſcience by his Spirit and word. Then you annex ſome things concerning the doctrine and conſent of the fathers and all wiſe men in all ages; but you propound them ſo doubtfully/ that (as touching our cauſe) we cannot perceive what your meaning is. Your wordes may ſo be underſtood/ as we moſt willingly conſent with you in this matter: agayne/ they may be ſo taken/ as we diſſent from you not a lytle/ nor without cauſe. We are perſwaded/ that ſeparation ſhould not be made from any Church/ eyther raſhly/ or at all ſo long as we may remayne with ſound fayth and cōſcience. You muſt therfore ſpeak more playnely/ what you think of our ſeparation/ if you ſuppoſe we have erred in this behalf: all thoſe things being diſcuſſed by the word of God/ which we have mencyoned in the preface and Confeſſion aforeſaid. In the meane tyme heare and ponder well (we pray you) what Mr. Beza that learned man and well deſerving of the Church of Chriſt hath wrytten and publyſhed ſome while ſince concerning this queſtion. Thus he hath in his epiſtles publyſhed/ in the eight epiſtle ſent to Ed: Grindall heretofore Prelate of London/ wherein wryting of the ſtate and corruptiōs of the Churche of England/ he ſayeth, If it be trew which is commōly reported, and wherof my ſelf am not yet perſwaded, that private Baptiſme is there permitted to women, I ſee not what is to turne back againe from whence men came, if this be not: &c. But if thoſe things be true, which I thincke are not lykely, to wit, that the Metropolytanes retaynē in vſe thoſe moſt filthy abuſes (then which the Church of Antichriſt hath not any thing more intollerable) namely, pruralyties of benefyces, lycences of non reſidency, licences to mary and eat fleſh, and other the lyke: this were certeinly (which I ſpeake with horrour) not a corruption of Chriſtianity, but a manifeſt defection from Chriſt: and therfore they not to be condemned, but commended rather, which oppoſe them ſelves to ſuch endevours, &c. Theſe and many other the lyke ſayings he hath in his epiſtles and other bookes publyſhed. Now as touching the things which he thought not to be ſo much as lykely, we know them to be moſt true: neyther thoſe only/ but almoſt an hundreth the lyke/ as we have touched in the preface of our Confeſſion. Among which we beſeech you conſider theſe three ſpecially (yet ſo as

you

you turne not your eyes away frō the rest) the confirmation of such as have bene
baptised (when nowe they are waxen older) administred by the Prelats themselves unto this day: Their holy Orders of Clergy: The discipline and sanctions of
the Cannō Law (as they call it) yet reteyned in that Churche: and tell us (we pray
you) freely and syncerely/ what now you think of the estate of that Church/ and
of our separation. Verily (if we conceive you right) your self expound the marke, the
name, and the nomber of the name of the Beast, to be understood of these three last
aforesaid abhomynations of Antichrist: In your exposition of Rev.13.ver,16.17.18.
And to receive these/ you know also well is forbydden unto all under payne of e-
ternall damnation. Rev.14.9.10.11. and 18.4.5.

But to returne to M. Beza agayne/ in him there are many thinges (cōcerning
our cause) to be carefully observed: first/ that his private epistles he set forth in
publyck: secondly/ that in the he did not dissemble/ but freely and ingeniously declare his iudgment of the estate of the Church of England: thirdly that yet he was
no busibody/ or unwise which would clime into this seate/ or by provoking that
church made his cause the worse with good mē etc. fourthly/ if ther were nothing
els/ yet by this we may well think/ that what you say of your self/ is not the answer of the other brethrē which are in any place in Churches and Vniversityes: lastly
that he should not have burst/ if he had dissembled these things/ nor yet while he
wrote thē godly and faythfully/ was factious vnciuill, or sowed any tares, but bare
witnes to the truth of the Gospel of Christ/ and did truly shew that he trod in the
steps of the Apostle who wryteth and testifyeth thus of himself and of all the faith
ful servāts of Christ/ we cānot do any thing against the truth, but for the truth. 2 Cor.
13.8. But these things by the way: Yet so as you may well consider with your self
(beloved Brother) whether the things which here and ther in your letter you seem
to insinuate against us/ fal not upō the very head of that most godly mā Mr. Beza
by lyke right/ or rather indeed by lyke wrōg. Of other lyke godly and learned mē
we will not now speake: it shall suffice here to have mencioned him alone. And
where you seem to acknowledg for true Pastors the Prelats and Priests by thē created (such as the English ministery is knowē to be) mynd how well you have done
this and how agreably with the Spirit of God/ which calleth such/ Locusts, false
Prophets, the whores marchants/ &c. But touching that which you speak of
Christ our Saviour how he brought iudgment to victory, not by crying out and filling the streets with clamours, but by blowing softly upon the smoking flax and handling tenderly the brused reed. This we do indeed most willingly acknowledg/ and
pray that we may alwayes followe this his most sacred example. Neverthelesse/
this also must be remembred/ that Christ dealt after one maner with the weack (of
whome here the speach is) after an other with the * Scribes and Pharisees and Mat.16.3.4
other the like sworne enemyes of the truth: such as at this day be the Prelats and and 23. cap.
their complices: which who is it that doth not know? who is it that doth not acknowledg. The same also may be seē in the Apostles of Christ and in their dealing
with Simon Magus, Elymas, Hymenæus, Alexander, Philetus, Diotrephes, &c.

Which things being so/ we humbly beseech you (reverend and beloved Sr.)
by that most holy name of Christ/ which you professe/ by the mercyes of God
wherewith he hath loved us in Christ/ that you would think of another course
(then such as yet it seemeth you allow) that you would take an other way for dis-
covering and destroying the defection of Antichrist/ for setting forward the salvation edificatiō/ and peace both of us and others. Hold on to defend the true fayth
(as now a good while you have done with great praise and fruit of the godly) and
discover errours: mayntayne good causes/ and forsake evill: Strive for Christ and
the truth of his Gospell/ and fight against Antichrist and the remnants of his
Apostasy. Let it be manifest to all/ what your mynd and iudgment is/ not only
concerning the fayth of Christ/ but also concerning the mystery/ Apostasy/ and
iniquity of Antichrist: ffinally/ as touching our selves in speciall/ if you wryte
agayne/ we do humbly and earnestly entreat/ if any where we have erred

in our

in our fayth and cause/ that you vouchsafe to shew it us by the light of Gods word. Otherwise it wil be suspected/ seing you bestow so much paynes in discussing these things which concerne the maner and not the matter it self/ that eyther you do dissemble your iudgment (what soever it be) or that in very deed you are of the same mynd with us: specially seing now you have wrytten/ that you do not any preiudice at all to our cause, and have spoken this religiously before the Lord.

Pity/ (we pray you) our Church, here exiled/ every where reproched/ eaten up in a maner with deep poverty/ despised and afflicted wel nere of al/ against which sathan hath now a long tyme attempted all utmost extremyties. Pity them, from whome we have departed, who under pretence of the Gospell contynew still in Antichristian defection/ and do so stifley hold and eagerly mayntayne it/ as there is scant any among them that dare so much as hisse against it. Pity these Churches (among whome we sejourne) in which wheter you look at the publyck prayers/ or the Administration of the Sacraments/ or the execution of discipline/ there be sundry tares, (if they may be called tares) or rather corruptions/ and those also not of small moment: at which/ as is reported/ the Anabaptists/ and others not a few that lyve here do stumble: of which also we have heretofore conferred frendly with the ministers of these Churches (men indeed learned and our bretheren beloved) but hitherto we do not accord therein: yet hope for better consent herafter/ by the blessing of God/ and throug the help of you and other godly men. Finally/ pity the whole Church of Christ, which verily it is not meet nor expedient neyther indeed ought/ among so many and grievous woundes of hers universally inflicted/ to be further galled with this particular wound/ that you should not take it in good part to have by us the true faith of Christ publyshed and the remnants of Antichrists Apostasy discovered.

And thus have we wrytten freely and boldly unto you/ good Sr. whom we do unfeynedly acknowledg to be godly/ learned/ and well deserving of the Church of Christ. For we had rather/ that men should fynd fault with our boldnes/ then that Christ should reprove us for leaving his cause. Neyther doubt we but your self according to your wonted and commendable humanity/ wil pardon us this fault/ whereinto we have ben drawen/ not with a mynd to contradict/ but with love of verity and affection of charity. And God himself even our father/ which hath loved and called us in Christ/ and hath given us eternall consolation and good hope through grace/ fulfill in you all the gratious pleasure of his goodnes and the work of fayth with power/ that the name of our Lord Jesus Christ may bee glorified in you/ and you in him. The grace of our God and Lord Jesus Christ be with your spirit. Amen.

From Amsterdam: the 19. of the second moneth/ called February/ 1599.

Yours in the Lord most addicted.

Francis Iohson.	Henry Ainsworth.
Daniel Studley.	Georg Knyveton.
Stanshall Mercer.	Christopher Bowman.

And the rest of the English people exiled for the Gospell sake and at this present remayning at Amsterdam.

To his beloved brethren the English people at Amsterdam.

Grace and peace from the Lord.

YOur Letters (loving Brethren) I received yesterday and read. If your messēger had shewed mee before, to whome, or whither I should have written, the matter had beene other wise caried: but I sought and wayted a whole moneth, being vncertaine to whom I might send. If any thing were done otherwise then we would, it was your owne fault. That ye giue no place to false suspition, I did nothing without the knowledge of my brethrē and Colleagues. To you I gave counsell: if it please you not, you may let it alone for me: it becommeth not vs to be contentious: for it is not our custome, nor the custome of the Churches of God. Now that Messenger of yours spake onely to me, without letters, and called not on any of my Colleages: What thē is the blame you lay vpō me? *none forbad me to give counsel alone. You asked indeed about a matter of faith, but wee thought good rather to deale about giving you cōsell. What? if a mā answere not according to your prescript, is it by and by an iniurie? Give vs leave, brethrē, I pray you, to use our own iudgement: we thought it fitter to give you counsell, then to make an answere to your demaundes, and that this wee might doe vnto you in brotherly dutie. If we might not, "yet will wee bee more indifferent towards yow: you may for vs abstaine, you may rent the Letters, and we also will concele it. I wrote as touching counsell, because I thought ther was need of it. I wrote not of the question, because I thought the time was not for it. Otherwise I had neuer thought of you, or your matters, no not so much as in my dreame: so greatly doe I shunne to bee a medler in other mēs matters. You will say, why was not the time for it? Surely because the matter was not cleere to me, to have beene handled in order, and good maner: Wher unto by giving you counsell, I called you backe. For if you kept good manner and order, yow might hav shewed it: if you kept it not, you might have returned vnto it and observe it. I knewe nothing at all, either by you, or by any other, which I speake, to the ende that you suspect none that is innocent. Our manner is to make answere in order, to them that aske according unto order: if any aske not in order, our manner is to call them backe to order, as is meete: yea if any vrge vs a hundred times besides order: we will call him backe an hundred times vnto order; or else by silence take order for our owne quietnesse and securitie. Will you therefore take the thing in question for graunted? Pardon me (deare brethren:) this is more thē either veritie or charitie doth teach. Hee that speaketh a thing different, speaketh neither

*Nemo vetuit ut solus consilium darem.

"Si non licuit nobis, at nos æquiores erimus erga vos: licet per nos abstinere, literas licet descindere, etiam nobis dissimulaturis.

this nor that " of the questiō: but he who vppon advice dooth speake a different thing, dooth deferre his iudgement, giving sentence on neither side If you will not permit mee to do this, which euerie man may lawfully doe, " I will take this one thing as my right, to keepe silence, that I may free my speach from cauillations. Hee that shall say " I cōfesse the thing, shall wittingly offend against the truth.

De questione.

Vnum mihi assumam pro jure meo, silentium, &c.

Qui me confessum dixerit in veritatem impinget sciens.

Others have set forth confessions. I know it, and I commend it: for eyther they seemed and were sayd to stagger in the hands of their persecutors, or else" moved of consciēce they did it orderly with the consend and approbation of the Church: but he who writeth with a mind to dissent, writeth against order, and sifteth the soares of the Church against the law of charitie. But you professe, that if there be any dissention, you do not dissemble it Surely in your confession I see no token wherby I may be certainely perswaded of it. Haue me excused: my senses are to dull to smell out things that are so secret. And yet now I thāke you euē for this, that you acknowledge your dissent in some things from the ministers of the Church of Amsterdam: and I thanke God which moued mee to suspend my iudgement. Therefore I did well who beeing altogether ignorant of your matters, did yet so write that I prevented a thing by you dissembled, (or at least obscurely set down) by whole some counsel.

Religione adducti.

The end, which is the cleering of your selves (although I knew nothing of you) you shall sooner attaine in one day by dealing with the Church wherein you are, then in an hundred yeare (if you should live so long) by writing to other Churches " hither and thither. You do not yet perswade me that you have dealt orderly: if we sticke constantly to order, and you dislike it, at least beare with vs. For whereas you say that you are euery where proclaimed heretikes, &c. I knewe nothing of you, neither should yet have knowne any thing if you had held your peace: so strongly are my eares stopped against al rumors. Of the fact of the English Churches, I have not certaine knowledge: why would you have vs speake? You might have been silent as I admonished you by my letters, and will you not let vs be so? " You may if so be you know the thing so well, have the iudgemēt of it with your selves: but to publish it among the people, to call for abettors of it, and to exact like judgement of vs you cannot Keepe your confidence to your selves, and leave vs our modesty, who have resolved not to speake of other mens matters, except we know them thoroughly. You thinke that other good mē will say otherwise, but I think better of them who in my perswasion are furnished with knowledge, skill, and wisedome from heaven, that they would sooner subscribe to our modestie, then to this your

Huc illuc.

Vos siquidē ita novistis probe, judicium penes vos habere potestis: Sed in vulgo id pronunciare, &c. non potestis.

your iudiciall confidence. To looke to the event, is a point of wisdome: which if you regard not, I pray God the author of all wisedome to give you discretion.

Touching the conclusion, (Bretheren) what shall I say otherwise then I haue said? I verily have resolved neither for you, nor for any mortall man to bee headie and inconsiderate in iudging: especially when it neither belongeth to me to do it, neither can it bee done with any fruit. If you can doe it rightly, wee doe not hinder you: but let vs who cannot, professe this one thing to you, that we can be no iudges. Touching others whome we knowe, we have spoken else where: but touching them, because we knowe thē not, " wee do not yet speak. Cōcerning *Beza* (how excellent a man) that which you often say, take heede Brethren, you bee not deceived. He spake by way of supposition, which you expresse in your letters: we, because we see, and experience doth teach vs, that his wordes being spoken by way of supposition, are vnderstoode of many as spoken simply, dare not so much as answere by way of supposition. Is this such an hainous and capitall fault with you? bee it farre from you Brethren, bee it farre from you to take that course with good men, which God, reason, and the times haue taught vs to be daungerous. Rash and headie iudgements are not to be required, nor to bee endured, not to be heard. That God of truth might iustly punish vs, if casting a side discretion (which is most needefull in these times) wee should answere alwayes to all questions according to the lawes prescribed by such as propounde the same. These three things according to God and vnder him are a lawe to vs, veritie, charitie, and discretion. If any one of these be wanting, we are afraid to offend. We crave of you (brethrē) that at least, you woulde leave vs this our religious feare, till all thinges bee made more plaine and easie vnto vs: and if you thinke your selves more strōg in iudging, beare with vs as with weake ones, til by godly quietnes and holy studie, we may attaine to more high and certaine thinges. That which wee may doe, truely, godlily, brotherly, wisely, we will neuer be slacke to doe, if wee may profite you and the Church of Christ. The Lorde furnish you (beloued Brethren) with his Spirit, and direct you to veritie and charitie in holy wisedome and faith to the glorie of his name, the edification of his bodie, and obtayning of your owne salvation, Amen.

Ne adhuc quidem dicimus.

Leyden, Wednesday, the 10. of March. 1599.

Yours vnfeynedly,
Fran. Iunius.

To the learned and our beloved Brother in Christ Mr. Francis Junius. at Leyden in Holland.

GRace and peace from God the Father and our Lord Jesus Christ Reverend Sr. your letters were delyvered vs: which when we had read / we thought thus with our selves: If we wryte againe / it wil be thought perhaps contentious / if we hold our peace it may prove hurtfull to the truth. What is then to be done? We must absteyne from contending yet so as the truth be not forsaken for which the Apostle exhorteth even to striue earnestly. Thus then (worthy Sr) receive our answer briefly. In that you did nothing in this matter, without the knowledg of your brethren and Colleagues, we therefore give you thanckes: for now you have had consultatiō together / yet shew you not any one errour in our fayth and cause. Touching that we rested not in your counsell, we had many and waighty reasons so to move vs which we signifyed to you in our former letters / but you have here in silence passed by them. Untyll you take them away / we think it cannot be shewed that in this matter we have done any thing otherwise then in good manner and order meet and needfull. Publyck infamy requireth publick apology.

Jude ver. 3

Others that have set forth / their Confessions, are by you acknowledged and commended We velyke only have offended in so doing: and that which every Church may lawfully do (and almost every man vpō iust cause) yet to vs and our Church you will not permit it. So indifferent are you towards vs, Neyther when they set forth their Confessions / did the whole Catholick Church consent: and if you speak of the consent and approbation of a particular Church / so also was our Confession publyshed But they wrote / dissenting from the Church of Rome and the like / being moved of conscience. And the very same thing have we lykewise done / dissenting from a daughter of the Romysh Church / touching her Leitourgy / hierarchy / constitution / to wit / the Church of England. Yet they thus wryting / neyther wrote against order, nor sifted the soares of the Church against the law of charity. No / nor we neyther. And touching the dissention not concealed, what need we wryte otherwise then as before we have done? It is with the Church of Englād / that we had and still have to deale in this behalf: and that difference we did by name and vnder certayn heades particularly relate: as both the thing it self and our exile did necessarily require. Now although in some thinges we differ from the ministers of these Churches / yet were they not before they despise admonition to be dealt with ** in lyke sorte. Else you might indeed some what rightly vrge order and the lawe of charity, if their names and peculiar descriptiō of that differēce had bē by vs particularly specifyed in that book. Neverthelesse whosoever know and consider the practise of these Churches (and of such only we speak) they may by that practise and our Confession cōpared together perceive there is difference betwene them and vs Yea we know that some have so observed. Otherwyse if it be as you pretend / that in our Confession you see not any token whereby you may be certainly persuaded there of, how is it that in so great agreement / they should by so many be judged as true Churches in the right fayth / we as heretickes? Besydes that even by this you do also graunt / that you see not but they consent in one with vs / touching the corruptions of the Church of England, and our separation from them: seing he that hath but half an eye may there see these most playnly propounded: In which behalf we give thancks both to you / and to God that hath brought you to give this judgment and testimony, For this is the very thing wherein we desyred your opinion. And by this appeareth also / how necessary it was for vs to set forth the Confession of our fayth (as now we have done) in respect of the Church of England / with which we have to doe / and from which for that we dissent / we are accused as hereticks and schismaticks / yll reported of and dryven into exile.

** There is one condition of a false church another of a true one (though corrupted) even till it despise admonition.

Touchinge the end, fact, and event, they being all in our former letters discussed /

we will now speake no more of them agayne: save this only / that in the Preface besydes other thinges we noted this / that we therfore publyshed the Confession of our fayth to the end the truth of God (what lay in us) might be cleared from reproch of men, and that others might be brought together with our selves to the same knowledg and fellowship of the Gospell. Of the lyke wrytings and acts of others approved by all the godly, we need say nothing. Neyther will we speake more of the many and grievous afflictions which for this fayth now a long tyme we have susteyned. Only we will mention (because you do thus urge us agayne) a litle booke wrytten by your self of your owne lyfe. In which you relate many troubles and afflictions which heretofore you have suffered for religiō sake / being pursued by the enemyes of Christ and his truth. Now if any should obiect against you / That many godly men knew not these things concerning you, neyther should yet have knowen them, if you had held your peace; that you have given place, and have passed over into another Court, that former injuryes, if any have bene, should by your self be borne in silence and hope, be forgiven by Christiā charity, to those from whom you received them, and hid from others by Christian wisdome, that there is no feare, least by so doing you should be burst, that every one should rather approve him self and his cause by duetyes of piety, and charity; then by outcryes and publyshing of wrytings, that the adversaries are not by this meanes made better; but more provoked by such a grievous sting: that you might, if so be you know the thing so well, have the judgment of it with your self, and not publysh it abreade, that you should not take up burthens of accusations, nor have judiciall confidence, that it is a point of wisdome, to look to the event: that rash and heady judgments are not to be required, not to be endured, not to be heard, &c. If any (we say) should object these thinges against you / which you do against us: would you not think it were unjustly done of thē? Why then do you that to others / which you would not have done to your self? Why urge you these thinges so unjustly against this Church of Christ and all the members of it / which hath suffered no afflictions of all sortes / no reproches / imprisonments / losses / banishments / deathes / then your self and divers other good men (yea though your troubles were tē tymes doubled) whose particular storyes notwithstanding are wrytten / publyshed / and approved. But we will let these thinges passe: for neyther do we lyke this course of aunting / disdayning / wynding away from the point in hand / so often used by you in your letters unworthely: Neyther do we deny but your aflictions were as you have related / heavy and to be lamented / which also / if you contynew faythfull to the end / the Captaine of our faith and beholder of our warfare will abundantly reward in the heavens / even Jesus Christ / to whome we commytt and commend this whole cause:

Vita D.F. Iunij, publyshed in the yeare 1595

The Conclusion also hath ben debated before. And now what others think of our cause / we referre to themselves eyther by silence to be insinuated / or other wise (as they think best) to be expressed. In the meane tyme we cannot omit M. Bezaes modest and yet confident judgment: whose supposition, because it is knowne to be of things most true and certayne / it is all one as if it had ben simply propounded. And thus to collect / we are perswaded is neyther to deale yll with good men / neyther hath God, reason or the tymes ever taught it to be daungerous. Nay / this rather do all these teach us to be full of daunger / whē as men are content to wink at the defection and remnants of Antichrist / and do not so much as by way of supposition beare witnes to the truth of Christ against them / being called into question. And here (if you please) ponder with your self the first originall of that Antichrist / his growth / his exaltation. Which Beza considering / judged them so daungerous / as in the same epistle he professeth / that it putteth him in great horrour and feare, as often as he thinketh of these things, and foreseeth the same or indeed more grievous punishments to hang over the heads of many people who at first did gladly recive the Gospell, frō which now by litle and litle they fall away. As touchinge our selves / we are not they who eyther can or will prescribe lawes unto others. We are of al men the meanest and weakest. And this we do freely and syncerely pro-

Bez. epis. 8.

ſyncerely profeſſe: and by all meanes we deſyre to abſteyne from to much confidence and to follow after an holy modeſty. And now of you (learned Sr.) and of other lyke godly/ learned/ ſtrong/ diſcreet men/ we deſyre to be inſtructed and informed/ yea to be brought agayne into the way/ if any where we be found to erre in our fayth and cauſe. This alſo do thoſe three things which according to God and vnder him ought to be a law to all men/ verity, charity, and diſcretion inſtantly call for at your handes. In which reſpect we exhort/ pray/ and beſeech you by the moſt ſacred name of Chriſt that you come to help the Lord among the mighty. Religious feare (which in all and every where is commendable) will nothing hinder this/ Nay it will further rather: whiles we cōſider that we are ſo to feare leaſt we offend/ as we do ſtill remember withall/ that God hath not gyven vs the ſpirit of fearefulnes/ but of ſtrength and love/ and ſoundnes of mynde: that we ſhould not be aſhamed of the teſtimony of our Lord/ neyther of them that be his priſoners/ exiles/ witneſſes. 2 Tim.1.7.8. Pardon (we pray you) that we wryte thus freely vnto you. The regard of the truth and love of you wringeth it from vs. For we are ſtudious of the truth of God/ and alſo of your name and eſtimation. If there be any thing wherein we may be ſerviceable vnto you without hinderance of the truth and love/ you ſhall commaund vs. And we truſt you will require nothing of vs otherwiſe. Farewell in Chriſt Jeſus: to whome we do hartely commend your holy and profitable labours and ſtudyes. Amſterdam: the 18, of March 1599.

Yours with entier affection in the Lord:

The brethren of the Engliſh Church at Amſterdam/ exiles of Jeſus Chriſt.

Another letter of the ſame Church to Mr·Francis Iunius, wherin their ſecond aforeſaid was included and ſent vnto him.

HEre included (learned Sir) we ſend the anſwer to your ſecond letter (longe ſynce delyvered vs) which we wrote the day after we had received yours: yet afterward thought we needed not ſend it (vnles ſome other occaſion were offered) both becauſe your ſelf intimated as if you would be ſilent/ if we wrote agayne/ and becauſe in very deed you did in thoſe letters yeeld vs the cauſe and anſwered nothing at all to any purpoſe/ eyther touching our Confeſſion of faith which was publyſhed/ or touching our former letters/ which we ſent vnto you thereabout. Of all which things/ now let the Reader judge. If you aſke/ why we chaunged our purpoſe/ and have now ſent you this letter/ which was wrytten ſo longe ſynce: lo here this litle booke included withall/ to witt/ your letters trāſlated into Engliſh and ſet forth in print. Whereupon we are conſtreyned/ not only to ſend theſe wrytten vnto you/ but to ſet them forth in publijck alſo in the Engliſh tounge. Yet let nothing here offend you: for it is we/ if any/ that are injuried/ yea and the truth it ſelf: inaſmuch as your firſt letter was publyſhed alone/ without our anſwer which you receyved from vs. By whoſe fault/ to what end/ with what equitie/ mynd you well. Sure that Prieſt which trāſlated yours/ wryteth in his preface (how truly you know) that your ſelf delyvered the copy of your firſt letter to a worſhipfull knight/ of whō he receved it/ and

turning

turning it into English imprinted it, yet have we not hitherto gyvē unto any so much as a copy eyther of yours or our owne: provyding (what we could) for your credyt, yea so, as we neglected our owne our selves, and were traduced by others, as now by this book publyshed will appeare unto all. But perhaps in this matter you purposed one thing, he another. Whatsoever it were, now you cannot but see, how the Prelats and Priests of our countrey do so interpret your letters, as if they had bene wrytten against the truth of the Gospell of Christ, which we professe, and for defence of the Antichristian Apostasy and tyranny, wherein they persist. Which thing we leave unto you, to be weighed seriously before the Lord.

Neyther is it to be omitted, that your private letters are set forth in publyck: yours (we say) who took it so yll that the Cōfession of fayth of this whole Church should be made publyck: who in these very letters of yours wrote so much of the publyck view, of publishing the woundes of the Church, undiscreetly, before so many deadly enemyes of God and the Church: of not offending any one of Christs disciples of not provoking Churches: of every one abounding in their owne sence, &c. It is marvell if your translatour turne not your owne wordes upon your self and tell you, that a Christian an humble and godly mynd ought to be otherwise affected, and setting a side the respect of their owne pryvate regard. &c. But this the more unjustly if he made your letters publyck without your knowledg. Which we indeed at first did suspect: tyll we saw your second Epistle come forth some while after the other. Neyther could we well thinke other wise of the matter, specially seing you wrote unto us, that we might rent the letters, and that you also would conceale it. Knowe moreover, that in the edition of your letters, there be certeyne clauses wherein the translation is not answerable to yours in Latine sent unto us: which we by your originall amend in our edition nowe ready to be published.

These (and many other things which yet we conceale) seem unto us to be of some moment. But we are deceived perhaps in our owne cause: and therfore you and your Translatour would, omytting all cōfutation, that others should have the iudgment therof: you in delyvering, he in publyshing your letters. But why then did you not vouchsafe to give us any knowledg therof? At least, why did you not so provide as that letter of ours which was in your handes, should also be translated and published? Did you thinck that * he which is first in his owne cause is iust? Why then did you not also mynd, that his neighbour comyng after him will make inquiry of him, that so both partyes being heard, iudgment may be gyven according to truth and equity? For which cause, though we have hytherto borne this, yet will we hereafter meet with such dealing by the best and fyttest meanes we can. Neither doubt we, but all these things (howsoever now they stand) will at length fall out for good both to us and to all other, which love Christ with all his ordinances, and hate Antichrist with all his abhominations. And having this hope, we will expect and endure whatsoever it shall please God who is the Lord and faythfull mayntayner of his servants.

* Pro. 18, 17 Consider here also your owne allegation out of Seneca before Pag. 35.

Concerning the differences (whereof you write agayne in your letters) which are betwene us and the dutch Church of this city, it needeth not that we wryte unto you of the particulars otherwise then as before we have donne. Yf you do yet desyre more we give you to understand that above a yeare synce we delyvered in wryting the true and particular narration of the whole matter, to the ministers and whole eldership of that Church: who (if yet they have not) may now communicate it with you By it also will appeare, that we have donne what was our duty, and as brotherly as we could. If not, let the errour be shewed and it shalbe corrected, God willing. In the meane tyme, because we are both pryvatly and publickly so much urged by you hereunto, we will briefely note the chief heades wherin we differ from them, and where about we have had dealing with them, both before and synce you wrote unto us.

They are these which follow:

The estate

1. The estate of the Dutch Church at Amsterdam: is so confused as the whole Church can never come together in one: the ministers can never together with the flock sanctify the Lords daye. the presence of the members of the Church cannot certeinly be knowen: and fynally no publick action whether excommunication or any other, can rightly be performed. VVhich is cōtrary to these Scriptures, 1. Cor. 12,27. and 11.20,23. Math. 18,17. with 1. Cor. 5,4. Act. 6. 2. 5. Numb. 8. 9, Act. 20,28.

2. They baptize the seed of them who are not members of any visible Church of whom moreover they have not care as of members, neyther admytt their parents to the Lords Supper. Gen. 17,7. 9. 10. 11. 1. Cor. 7,14. Exod. 12.48. with 2. Chron. 30,6. &c. Numb. 9. 13, Hos. 2,2,4. with Rev. 17,1. Ezech 16,59, &c.

3. In the publyck worship of God, they have devysed and use an other forme of prayer besydes that which Christ our lord hath prescribed Mat. 6. reading out of a book certayne prayers invented and imposed by man. Exod. 20,4,5. and 30,9. with Psal 141,2. and Rev. 8,3. Lev. 10,1. Esa. 29,14. with Mat. 15. 9. Rom. 8,26, Eph. 4. 8. 1. Pet. 2,5.

4. That rule and commandement of Christ, Mat. 18,15,16.17. they neyther observe, nor suffer rightly to be observed among them.

5. They worship God in the Idol temples of Antichrist. Exod 20,4. with Deut. 12,2,3. 2. King. 10,26. 27,28. and 18,4. Act 17,23. Rev. 18,11,12, &c.

6. The Ministers have their set mayntenance after another manner then Christ hath ordeyned, 1. Cor. 9,14. And that also such as by which any Ministery at all, whether popish or other what soever, might be mayntayned.

7. Their elders chaunge yearly and do not continewe in their office according to the doctrine of the Apostles and practise of the Primitive Churches. Rom. 12,4, 5,6,7,8. 1. Cor. 12,11,12, &c. Act. 20. 17. 28. 1. Pet. 5,1. 2. 3. 4. See also Numb. 8. 24 &c.

8. They celebrate Mariage in the Church, as if it were a part of the Ecclesiasticall administration, wheras it is in the nature of it merely civill. Ruth. 4. chap.

9. They use a new censure of Suspension, which Christ hath not appointed. Mat. 28. 20. Gal. 3. 15. 2. Tim. 3. 16. 17.

10. They observe dayes and tymes, consecrating certeyn dayes in the yeare, to the Nativity, Resurrection, Ascension of Christ, etc. Exod. 20. commaundement, 2. and 4. Rev. 1. 10. 1 Cor. 16. 1. 4. 2. Act. 20. 7. Col. 2. 16. 17. Esa. 66,23, Gal 4. 10. 11.

11. They receive unrepētant excommunicates, to be members of their Church: which by this meanes becommeth one body with such as be delivered unto Sathā. 1. Cor. 5. 5. 1. Tim. 1. 20.

These (among other) are the corruptions of the church aforesaid; which they are neyther able to defend, nor willing to forsake. Herein therfore we differ from them as they which knowe this estate of theirs may perceive by our confession compared with their errours noted before: which the Lord give them to see and mend. And for your self (good Sir) take you heed in goodlynes, that in this cause you do not in any respect withhold the duty which you ow unto them, or defence which you ow unto the truth. So let God almighty also love you, and Christ our Saviour be mercifull unto you. And this you may do truly, Godlye, brotherly, wisely with great profit to us and the Church of Christ every where. Therfore we exhort and beseech you in the lord that you be carefull alwayes to help (no way to hurt) the Church and cause of Christ, by your studyes, endevours, labours: which being thus directed the Lord Jesus blesse to the glory of his name, and your owne comfort for ever. Amen. Amsterdam.

The first day of the seventh moneth called July. 1602.

Yours in Christ, by whose grace we witnesse the truth of his Gospell, against the will-worship and remnants of Antichrist what soever:

Francis Iohnson. Henry Ainsworth. Daniel Studley.
Stanshall Mercer. Christopher Boman. Thomas Bishop.
David Bresto. With the rest of the brethren of the English Church now living as straungers at Amsterdam.

A third letter, written by Mr. Iunius, vpon receipt of the last aforesaid, and of his tvvo former imprinted before in England, and therevpon by vs sent vnto him included withall.

To his beloved brethren in Christ the English people at Amsterdam.

Salutations in Christ.

AN huge bundell of letters, beloved brethren, I received from you yesterday in the evening. I gave you counsell to rest from questiõs: you commaund me to enter into questions. I continew still in my purpose: for I esteem more of peace in the Church then of the seeds of strife: they that are fedde with these seeds, shall reap the fruit. Where you conclude and pronounce that I do therefore assent vnto you, it is a false conclusion: As towching the matter I have enjoyned my self silence: and although I be an hundred tymes called vpon by letters, I will continew still in the argument of counsell till I see another course taken. If it like you not, let it alone: neyther do I like the handling of questions in this tyme. It is more according to God that I be silent from questions in this estate of things, then that I powre forth my self and you together into them. You move many things in your letters, I wil rest frõ those things, and will occupy my self religiously in the work of the Lord. Christian wisdome will never suffer me to speak of questiõs controverted, the one party being vnheard.

That my letters vnto you, were translated into English, I have now first knowen it by you: I knew not that it was done. You object that my letters were not shewed by you. I beleev it: for both by letters and reports of many I have ben certifyed that they were not shewed. If it please you, shew them, for me you may. All shall see, how false reports have ben given forth concerning thẽ. I neyther am ashamed of them, neyther ever will be. But I pitty you (I speak it vnfeynedly) who for my letters give forth in publick your conclusions. With good men good dealing should be used. That the copyes of my letters were carryed into England, your selves may easily cõjecture, by what meanes it came to passe. About tẽ moneths synce, the Soveraign Quenes Ambassadour was there and two of your company dined with him. What hapned at that dinner you can remember. He came hither vnto me: he marveled at the fact of your departure: I told him that I had writtẽ vnto you, he desired a copy. To you I gave counsell: whosoever gave it forth in publick, hath done it without my knouwledg: I will not answer for an others doing, but for

 myne

myne owne. In the meane while I will pray God that he frame your mynds vnto the truth, wisdome, love, and peace, and all our mynds vnto his glory. Farewell in the Lord. From Leyden in Holland.

The 16. day of Iuly. 1602.

Yours vnfeynedly, Fr. Iunius.

The Answer to Mr. Iunius his third letter.

To the reverend and our beloved brother in Christ Mr. Fr. Iunius at Leyden in Holland.

Grace and peace in Iesus Christ.

YOur third and very brief letter (beloved Sir) we received this last week. They were your letters imprinted and included that made the huge bundell, if so it were. It is not well said of you / that terme the Confession of Christian faith and defēce of publishing it, to be questiōs and seeds of strife, nor that you say, we cōmand you to enter into questions. For the conclusion, whether it be true or false, now let others judge, which shall see your letters together with ours. Towching the matter, you have enjoyned your self silence. Yea and towching the maner and other things also, where you can fynd no answer neyther. Yet for the matter it self if so be that with the Papists, Anabaptists, or any the like we did erre frō the true faith, we doubt not but you would open your mouth to answer / to refute, to convince. But because in our faith you can shew no errour / and yet in this tyme and estate of things like not to stand for vs and this cause, it is safest to be silent. Wisely done in deed, but not according to God / who denoūcing by the Prophet hath said,
Ier.48.10. Cursed be he that doth the worck of the Lord fraudulētly, and cursed be he that kepeth
Psa.137.8.9 back his sword from blood: On the contrary / Blessed be he that shall reward thee, as
thou hast rewarded vs, ô daughter of Babel to be destroyed: Blessed be he that shall take and scattering dash thy children against the stones. If this against Moab and the materiall Babylō / how much more against Antichrist and the spirituall Babylon with al the daughters and abominatiōs thereof? If this against the shadow and type, how much more against the substance and body it self? Of the argument of counsell ynough is said. If you repeat it a thousand tymes, and yet take not away our answer and reasons / alledged in our first letters / we will alwayes repeat the same answer againe. Those many things which are conteyned in your letters and ours, do now come forth in publick. Neyther doubt we but this is the work of the Lord. See therefore that you be occupied therein religiously. That any should speak of things controverted, we desier not otherwise then the reformed Churches and those godly mē and Martyrs of Iesus, who with like purpose have published their confessions of faith and causes of their troubles, being so constreyned.

That your letters were not shewed by vs, we wrote not: but this, that we gave not a copy of them to any: for what cause, we wrote in our former. Shewed they were and read in the publick meeting of our Church. If your mynd were to have them shewed to others that knew we not. But now that you write this is your mynd / we shall shew them together with ours publickly vnto all. And if any have givē forth any false reports concerning them, let thē now be ashamed. In the meane time your self provided, by sending yours at first vnsealed / that they should be shewed to others, and be read also of others, before vs. Neyther doth it excuse the matter, which you wrote in your second / that the messenger shewed you not to whōe r whither you ſhould have written, and that therefore you ſought and wayted an whole moneth, being vncertayne thereof. For we did ſignify both theſe expreſſely in the Epiſtle dedicatory prefixed before that book which by the meſſenger was delivered vnto you. Els how knew you at the moneths end more thē before whither and to whō to ſend? Or when you knew / why did you not ſeale your letters? Was it becauſe you would have thē ſhewed? We beleev it: as alſo that for the ſame cauſe / the copyes of thē were caryed into England. And this too we knew / before they were tranſlated in Engliſh: but we held our peace / wayting to ſee what would follow therevpon. Now your ſelf ſee they are tranſlated and given forth in publick. For them therefore and with them / we trāſlate and publiſh ours: by which will appeare that we have dealt well with good men. You may call them as you pleaſe: it ſkilleth vs litle: this is the very thing we deſier and endevour / that the ſimplicity of the Goſpell of Chriſt / the iniquity of the defectiō of Antichriſt / may more and more be made knowen vnto all. If for this thing you pity vs, we will beare it: praying that God in Chriſt would pitty you. Where you write / that two of our company dined with that honorable Ambaſſadour / it is not true / that we know of. Neyther can we tell / what hapned at that dinner. He ſent not for vs to come vnto him / neyther did we like to intrude our ſelves. If by vs he would have ben certifyed of our cauſe / we would have done it willingly and ſyncerely. And you alſo / when he demaunded of you / might have ſhewed our letters with your owne / and the cōfeſſion of our faith / and given alſo copyes of both the letters. So might the Tranſlatour have given forth both in publick. So had you provided / that ſentence ſhould not be given / the one party being vnheard. Which thing Chriſtian wiſdome, your ſelf ſay, ſuffreth not to be done in queſtions controverted. In this behalf therfore you have erred / and this by you is to be anſwered: notwithſtāding that for his doing / himſelf is to anſwer / that tranſlated and publiſhed yours without your knowledg. For our ſelves / if any where we erre / ſhew it (we pray you agayne and agayne) by the word of God / that is / by the onely rule of truth / and we ſhal yeeld moſt willingly. And thus we pray God that he would guyde you together with vs and all his alway vnto Jeſus Chriſt / and that he would keep vs in him / who onely is the way, the truth, and the life. Whoſe name be bleſſed for ever. Amen. Amſterdam. July 21. 1602.

Yours in the truth and peace of the Goſpell of Chriſt:

F. Io. H. Ainſ. D. St. S. Mer.
C. Bom. T. Biſ. D. Bre.

Together with the other brethren of the Engliſh Church at Amſterdam.